Country Elegance
Projects for Woodworkers

Country Elegance
Projects for Woodworkers

Edward A. Baldwin

TAB BOOKS
Blue Ridge Summit, PA

FIRST EDITION
FIRST PRINTING

© 1991 by **Edward A. Baldwin**
Published by TAB Books.
TAB Books is a division of McGraw-Hill, Inc.

Library of Congress Cataloging-in-Publication Data

Baldwin, Edward A.
    Country elegance : projects for woodworkers / by Edward A. Baldwin.
        p.   cm.
    Includes index.
    ISBN 0-8306-0579-7   ISBN 0-8306-0527-4

    1. Woodwork.   I. Title.
TT180.B22   1991
684′08—dc20
                                                    91-4974
                                                    CIP

TAB Books offers software for sale. For information and a catalog, please contact TAB Software Department, Blue Ridge Summit, PA 17294-0850.

Acquisitions Editor: Kimberly Tabor

This book is dedicated to:
The memory of Dorothy Lillian Baldwin (nee Frier).
A wonderful mother and friend.
A person who left this world a better place
for her having been in it.

Contents

Preface   ix
Acknowledgments   xi

Woodworking Tips and Techniques	1
Country Footstool	13
Sweetheart Mirror	19
Combination Magazine Rack and Tissue Dispenser	23
Birdhouse Cookie Jar	29
Checkerboard Game and Coffee Table	37
Sweetheart Shadow Box and Change Holder	45
Mirrored Candle Sconces	49
Paper Cup Dispenser	55
Plate and Cup Rack	59
Teddy Bear Settle/Toy Chest	63
Curved Back Chairs and Rockers	71
Corner Shelves	83
Child's Rocking Chair/Doll Cradle Combo	89
Sweetheart Door Harp	99
Kitchen and Patio Chopping Block/Serving Cart	105
Sweetheart Settle	119
Rolltop Bread Box	127
Bunny Bandit and Calico Gal Wall Hanging	135
Game Table/Cabinet	141
Sweetheart Magazine Rack	149
Blanket Chest	153
Early American Dry Sink	161

Lap Desk   169
Deacon's Bench and Chest Combination   173
Tulip Motif Breakfast Nook   181
Forever Calendar Clock   195
Country Modern Grandfather Clock   201
Hanging Sweetheart Lamp   211
Tavern Lantern and Sconce   221
Corner China Chest   229
One Final Note   239

Index   241

Preface

While I was developing the projects for this book, I was pressured by many of my friends to define what Country Elegance meant. To put it slightly differently, what is country, much less Country Elegance?

Country Elegance is not a definitive style like Italian Modern or French Provincial. It's actually a feeling. Antique buffs define it in terms of joints and the kinds of fasteners and hardware used. Interior decorators will say it creates a warm glow and emanates an aura of basic simplicity.

My definition is somewhat different. To me, Country Elegance is livable, useful stuff, be it furniture or decorations. It is furniture that is functional and is something that looks better with age, the kind of stuff you put next to the fireplace, sink into or prop your feet on.

Country Elegance is an upbeat variation on traditional country in that its designs are unique and different. It is not necessarily the traditional styles or shapes of Early American or Colonial Furnishings, yet it provides the same feeling with a touch of class. Nothing in this book was made or intended to look like a replica of furniture.

The designs contained in this book are classical new designs that employ new woodworking techniques and blend basic craft ideas with woodworking. Some of the pieces are very basic and simple to construct. Some projects fall into the category of finewoodworking and require some basic skills to construct.

I think one of the greatest rewards for making projects such as the ones contained in this book is the knowledge that some of them will survive a long time, perhaps to be admired and appreciated by descendants, young people we may never know.

Acknowledgments

Project Design . . . . . . .Ed Baldwin
Editorial Director . . . . .Barbara Sachs Kremer
Decorative Folk Art. . . .Glennda Suter
Photography . . . . .Eddie Arthur
Art . . . . .Baldwin Productions
Choreographer . . . . . . .B. J. Stiemle
Production . . . . .Shirley Fischer
Sawdust Cleanup . . . . . .Mark Baldwin

The projects in this book were made using tools supplied by
Makita with router bits and saw blades supplied by Freud.

Woodworking
Tips and Techniques

Although the inspiration for many of the projects contained in this book was the warm utilitarian furniture built by hand in the early days of our country, the construction techniques employed to build these projects were thoroughly modern. These techniques included the use of modern adhesives, current day hardware and power tools both hand-held and stationary. As a basic premise I used simple glue joints secured with nails or screws or new spline techniques strengthened with recessed nails or screws. This is in stark contrast to the old days when complex joints were required because of archaic adhesives, and when nails and screws were not always available and time was abundant.

This approach may disappoint some of you who practice the time-honored techniques of traditional wood joinery and who may be looking for lapped goose-neck mortise and tenon joints with stubbed tenons locked with V-wedges. Sorry about that. However, for those of you primarily interested in building sturdy, handsome furnishings for your homes in a time-efficient manner, this book is going to save you money and show you some really neat ideas. Any of the projects contained herein can be modified to accommodate traditional techniques if you so wish. Those of you who frequently construct halved rabbetted oblique scarf joints will no doubt know where to put them!

Following are brief discussions of some of the various woods, chemicals, materials and tools I used. You will note I avoided the use of hide glue, casein glues, lacquer finishes, and the like. I opted to use the more up to date, current products that are easily available, easy to apply and perform well.

HOW TO SELECT WOOD

Walking into today's home centers can sometimes be a disappointment when it comes to selecting wood. Most of the white woods, pine etc., are usually not straight and perfect, are loaded with knots and imperfections. Yet they want an arm and a leg for the stuff. The hardwoods in most cases are laminations and likewise carry a hefty price. Depending on where you live, there will always be an abundance of one certain kind of wood that is generic to your area. For example, redwood may be plentiful in California, but here in the Midwest where I live, good heart redwood is not in abundance. Sometimes you can get a bargain by buying certain low grades of wood and ripping the boards to obtain good stock. Then by laminating the good boards you can make good larger stock from which to make furniture.

Getting to know someone who owns a sawmill is highly advised if you are into serious woodworking. Finding mail-order houses that offer good deals on certain plywoods and hardwoods is also advised. If you own land with lots of trees, you can always cut your own, but it takes forever to air-dry most woods.

Generally speaking, woods are divided into two general categories: hardwood lumber, which comes from deciduous trees (the ones that shed their leaves every year) and softwood lumber, which comes from conifers (evergreens). Hardwoods are harder to cut and work with and are usually more expensive than softwoods. Conversely, hardwoods make more durable and longer lasting furniture than softwoods.

Common hardwoods include red and white oak, walnut, pecan (which is usually hickory in disguise), ash, elm and maple. Softwoods include redwood, fir, cedar and pine (both white, which is a soft fine grain wood, and yellow, which is almost hard enough to be considered a hardwood). Douglas fir is a particularly good softwood to work with. Softwoods vary widely in their tendency to shrink, swell, and warp. The most stable of softwoods are redwood, pine and cedar. Newly cut wood has a lot of moisture and sap and needs to be seasoned by air and kiln drying. Wood that is not seasoned will warp, crack and shrink.

When you are choosing lumber, look at the ends of the boards to check the direction of the growth rings. Heartwood is cut from the center of the tree and has dense growth rings, which produce a highly rot-resistant

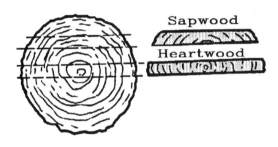

board. It may become thinner as it loses moisture, but it is not as likely to crack and warp as sapwood which is cut farther from the center of the tree. Sapwood is more likely to be vulnerable to rot and insect damage.

WOOD GRADES

Lumber is graded according to overall quality of the board. This rundown will give you an idea of the categories of wood. I think your best bet is to take your project plans to your lumber dealer, show him what

you want to make and perhaps he can assist you in your selection of wood. Remember you don't need to buy the highest grade of lumber for every project.

#4 Common - Low in cost and with lots of imperfections. Prone to crack (check) along the grain. Good for fences or projects where appearance is not crucial.

#3 Common - Small knotholes are common, are easily dislodged while you work, and tend to become flying missiles when cut. Wood is prone to check (crack).

#2 Common - Contains some small knots, fairly clear, good for paneling and flooring and outdoor projects.

#1 Common - Contains some small tight knots and other insignificant imperfections; is the top grade of the regular board grades.

D Select - Comparable to #1 common but better seasoned and more expensive.

C Select - A few small blemishes on one side of the board, the other side is usually clear and almost perfect.

1 & 2 Clear - The best and most expensive grade of wood. Only used for the finest furniture and cabinets.

WOOD JOINING

This is an area where fine woodworking buffs get persnickety about the proper ways of putting boards together. You really can use the simpler joining techniques combined with glues and fasteners to make the projects in this book. Mitered joints, tongue and grove or fancy dovetails are simply not necessary to build these projects, nonetheless:

Butt Joints: A butt joint connects the end or edge of one piece to the surface, edge or end of another. This is an extremely weak joint and needs to be strengthened with splines, nails, screws, dowels or other reinforcement. This is an ideal joint for putting narrow boards together to form larger boards. To minimize warpage, assemble the boards with the grain of every other board inverted as shown.

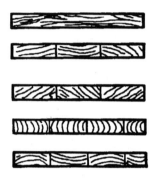

Rabbets: This is not referring to a cute little bunny rabbit but rather a joint that is formed by cutting mating joints that provide a larger area for glue than a common butt joint. This creates a stronger joint and is especially useful for cabinet, base, drawer and box construction. It is commonly reinforced with nails or screws. A rabbet joint also has other uses such

BUTT JOINTS

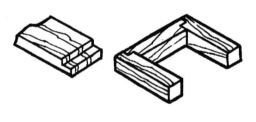
RABBET JOINTS

as recessing the inner surface of a door inside the door opening.

Lap Joints: A lap joint is used to connect two members at right angles. The two surfaces are flush and provide a large surface area for glue.

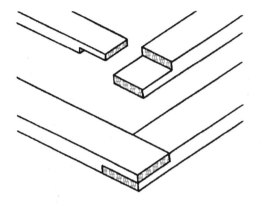

Dadoes: A dado is a groove that accommodates another member. There can be several different kinds of dado joints. A through dado extends all the way from edge to edge; a stopped dado extends from one end to a point short of the opposite edge; a blind dado is like a tendon and is stopped short of both edges.

Mortise and Tenon Joints: There are many variations on the basic concept of this type joint. The common garden variety is shown here. This is an extremely tough and durable joint. It can be made very strong with the use of wedges and pegs. An unglued joint like this is good to use for furniture you may wish to disassemble.

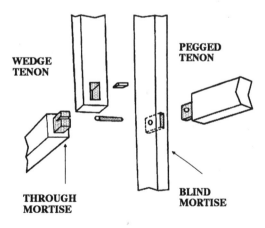

MORTISE AND TENON JOINTS

Miters and Bevels: Most picture frames contain mitered ends. Put simply, a miter joint connects two

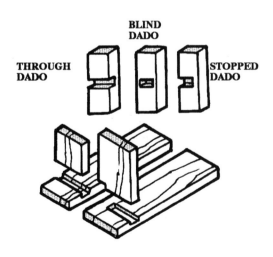

DADO JOINTS

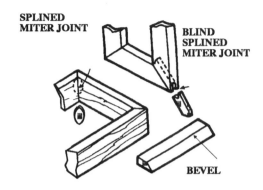

SPLINED MITER JOINT

BLIND SPLINED MITER JOINT

BEVEL

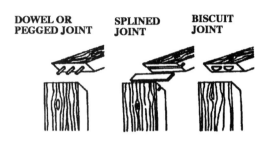

DOWEL OR PEGGED JOINT

SPLINED JOINT

BISCUIT JOINT

MITERS AND BEVELS

angle cut ends concealing the end grain of the wood in the process. The most common miter is a 45-degree cut, used to construct right angle assemblies. A flat miter is made across the width (surface) of the board. An on edge miter is made across the end (thickness) of the board. A bevel miter is an angle cut made along an edge or surface.

Splines, Dowels and Biscuit Joinery: Joints can be reinforced with the use

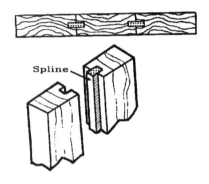

Spline

SPLINED GLUE JOINT

of dowels, splines and biscuit splines. Screws also can be used. Dowels require the use of a drill bit and a doweling jig. Regular splines are strips of wood inserted into slots or dadoes cut into the ends of wood joints, usually as a saw kerf. Biscuit

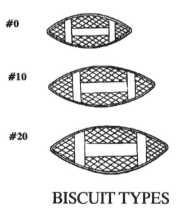

#0

#10

#20

BISCUIT TYPES

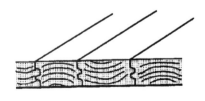

GLUE JOINT

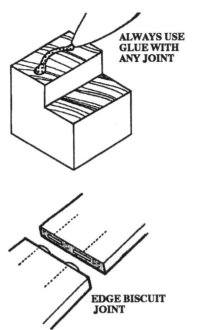

ALWAYS USE
GLUE WITH
ANY JOINT

EDGE BISCUIT
JOINT

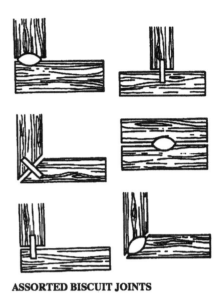

ASSORTED BISCUIT JOINTS

splines require the use of a special biscuit slot cutter or a router with a spiral or veining bit or a slot cutter bit.

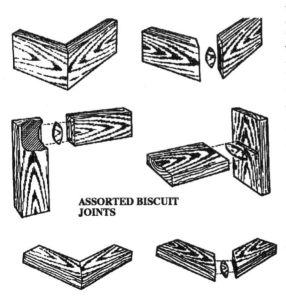

ASSORTED BISCUIT
JOINTS

Of the methods discussed, biscuit splines are probably the most effective since the splines swell when glued into the slot and make for a tight and effective joint bindery. Recessed screws are the next choice when used in conjunction with an adhesive. Regular splines are the next choice, followed by wood dowels, which are the weakest of the choices. Splined joints may be left unglued if the assembled boards will be secured at the ends or edges. This allows for the boards in the assembly to expand and contract with changing atmospheric conditions and helps prevent warping and cracking.

Biscuit splines offer the most flexibility when joining wood in various positions as shown.

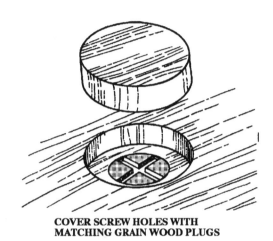

COVER SCREW HOLES WITH MATCHING GRAIN WOOD PLUGS

Adhesives: I recommend both glue and fasteners (screws, nails, bolts, dowels, splines or biscuit splines) for all joints, unless you want to be able to disassemble the joint at a later time. Aliphatic resin, a cream/yellow-colored glue commonly sold as Titebond or carpenter's glue, is best for most indoor projects. In some cases a two part epoxy and a clear silicone glue work best for projects designed to be used both inside and outdoors. A marine glue and epoxy is best for most outdoor projects.

Clamping is necessary for all glued projects. The important thing to remember is to hold the pieces together firmly. You don't need to clamp so tight as to force the glue out of the joint. Projects that are going to get a lot of stress should be clamped overnight. While most yellow-glued projects are ready to go in about an hour, the additional clamping time is good insurance.

Hardware: All indoor projects should be made with hardware of brass, bronze, aluminum or alloyed steel. Most brass screws, however, are weak and will snap very easily, especially when used in hardwood, even with predrilled screw holes. I suggest you use the screws provided with the brass hardware with extreme caution. Alloyed steel screws that look like they are brass would be the best choice. Modern steel fasteners are okay for indoor projects. However, all steel contains carbons, and, if the steel becomes wet or is used in a very humid condition, the steel deteriorates and will cause black spots to form on your project. Galvanized products are better; however, galvanized coatings have been known to break down and should be coated with a rust inhibiting product. Uncoated or untreated steel hardware should never be used for outdoor projects.

Screws and Nails: To prevent splitting the wood, drill a pilot hole for each screw and for nails in some cases. Use a drill bit slightly smaller in diameter than the screw shank. For a finished look, all screws should be recessed or countersunk and covered over with wood plugs. Plugs can be cut from matching wood stock with the use of a plug cutter. This type of plug can match the wood grain and blend in with your wood surface. Wood plugs can also be cut from wood dowels, but they represent end grain and will be more apparent, especially if you stain your project.

Finishing nails should be toenailed or recessed below the wood surface

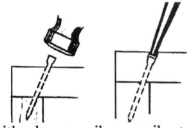

with a larger nail or a nail set. Fill the recessed nail hole with wood filler or a paste made from sawdust and glue.

The kinds of screws I use for most woodworking projects are either Phillips head or square head type that are self-tapping carbon steel. For exterior projects Dacrotized or galvanized screws should be used. Another kind of screw that combines the features of both a square and a

Phillips head is also a good choice for woodworking projects. The one screw that should only be used with extreme caution is the old-fashioned slotted screw. Many a screwdriver has slipped off of this kind of screw, thereby ruining a wood-working project.

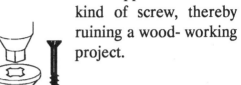

PRESERVATIVES AND FINISHES

Preservatives are not a consideration for interior projects. However, if you plan to use any of these projects outdoors a preservative is an absolute necessity. The two major causes of wood deterioration are decay and insect damage. Some woods—cedar and redwood—are naturally insect resistant, primarily the heartwoods. Sapwood, redwood and cedar however, can fall victim to decay and insect damage. Pressure-treated lumber is the best choice for exterior projects. But, if you insist on using other woods, then you need to find a good preservative, and there are many good products available.

Penetrating stain/sealer is available in many different tones and provides the convenience of staining and sealing in one application. It enhances the grain and color of the wood, and provides depth of color rather than a flat finish, such as paint, which covers up the wood grain. If you insist on a flat finish, a top coat of varnish will do. Use a good marine grade. Apply a thin first coat and then a full strength second coat.

For interior projects use a good finish sealer stain or a combination of sealer, stain and paint. Softwoods are exceptionally hard to deal with since the surface of the wood is very porous. Staining can sometimes cause strange results in the wood taking the stain too dark in spots. Thus it is necessary to seal softwoods before staining them to obtain a uniform look.

Hardwoods on the other hand, work well with stain sealers and take the chemicals rather uniformly. An excellent product for hardwoods is a Danish oil stain sealer, a resin that flows into the pores of the wood and over time swells, filling the wood fiber and providing a hard surface to resist water stains, food spills, etc. It's easy to apply with a rag or steel wool, and the results are quite predictable.

We used a form of Swedish tole painting over the finished surfaces of some of the projects in this book. The paint we used was a water-based acrylic.

The stains and varnishes used on these projects were all solvent and oil based.

WORKING WITH PATTERNS

It is extremely difficult to write a projects book and include full size drawings. Hence we use scale drawings most of the time. A scale drawing always appears on a background grid of small squares with a legend that specifies the scale. For instance, a common scale is one square grid on the scale equals one square inch.

You can copy this design to your wood one square at a time or you can use a pantograph. This device can be adjusted to copy the design from the scale drawing to a full size drawing

on your wood board via a stylus and several rods that can be adjusted to various sizes. However, this is a lot of work, and most people don't own a pantograph.

The simplest and easiest way to get a full size drawing from a scale drawing is to go to your local copy center and use a copying machine that makes enlargements. The largest size paper these machines will use in most cases is 11" by 17", but you can make as many sheets as you need to get the whole pattern, even if it's in pieces.

Identical parts should be made using the first part you made as the pattern. This approach is especially helpful when you have to drill holes that require perfect alignment.

This pretty much summarizes the nitty gritty stuff, so let's go make some projects!

NOTES AND CALCULATIONS:

Country Footstool

This country classic is unique in that it has legs that take on the flair of inverted cabriole legs, something very French. Yet this is only 1" lumber inverted to look that way. This is a very simple design and easy to make.

MATERIALS

¾" red oak 6" x 120"
  8 pieces 4½" x 11" legs
  4 pieces 2¼" x 9" leg spacers
  2 pieces 4" x 16½" long support
  2 pieces 4" x 8½" short support

¼" plywood 16½" x 16½" cushion base

HARDWARE AND MISCELLANEOUS

  1 piece foam rubber 2" thick
    16½" x16½" cushion
  1 piece upholstery fabric 24" x 24"
  Small bottle of carpenter's or
    Titebond glue
  24 screws 1¼"
  4 screws 1"
  Splines ¼" x ¾" cut to size
    (biscuit splines optional)
  24 wood plugs ½" red oak
  1 pint Danish oil, dark walnut

TOOLS REQUIRED

  Drill with ½" countersink bit
  Router with cove, rounding over
    and slot cutter bits
  Biscuit joiner (optional)
  Screwdriver
  Table saw
  Saber saw (band saw preferable)

  Pipe clamps 24" or longer
  Stapler with ¼" staples
  Flap wheel sander
  Web clamp

INSTRUCTIONS

While I show miter cuts for the legs and the use of splines, there are alternate forms of construction you may wish to use. Butt joints instead of miters are acceptable and plain butt gluing instead of cutting splines may be ok if you use screws from the sides into the center support to hold it all together. To obtain a long lasting project, however, the techniques as shown are preferable.

1. Measure and cut all of the wood pieces to size. The leg miters should be cut first by ripping a four foot length of wood 4½" wide at a 45 degree angle and then cutting the legs to length of 11". The last step is cutting the leg shapes. The splines should be cut so that the thickness is a hair under ¼" and make certain the grain runs the width of the spline, not the length.

2. Using a router with a ¼" slot cutting bit, cut the spline openings as shown. Make absolutely certain that the cutter is set in the exact center of the ¾" lumber or you will

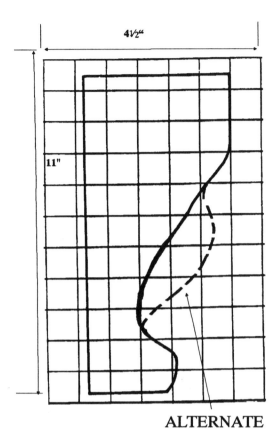

4½"

11"

ALTERNATE

pull your hair out when assembly time comes since the boards will

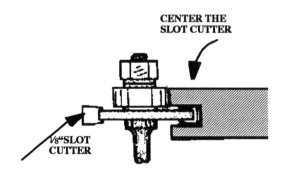

CENTER THE
SLOT CUTTER

⅛"SLOT
CUTTER

THIS SETTING IS INCORRECT

not be flush. Using a router table will make this job easier.

3. Assemble the center support first.

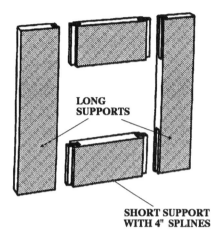

LONG
SUPPORTS

SHORT SUPPORT
WITH 4" SPLINES

SEAT BASE

Use splines and glue and clamp the assembly securely with bar or pipe clamps.

4. After the center support glue has set up, lay it on a flat work surface supported by some 1" wood blocks in each corner. Assemble the legs, leg spacers and splines. Using glue and the splines, assemble four leg and spacer assemblies.

5. Turn the assemblies upside down and place them around the center support, using glue on the center support sides. Pull the whole as-

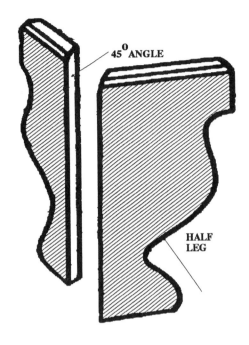

45° ANGLE

HALF LEG

LEG ASSEMBLY

6. While the glue is still moist drill a countersink hole into the bottom side of each leg approximately 2" from the leg bottom ⅜" from the edge of the miter cut. Make certain you do this carefully and keep the miters at a perfect alignment while the hole and screw hole is drilled. Immediately screw a screw into place pulling the wood pieces tightly together. Do this again on

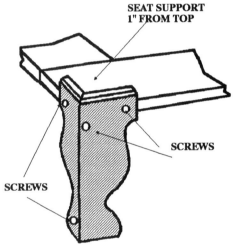

SEAT SUPPORT 1" FROM TOP

SCREWS

SCREWS

sembly together using a web clamp wrapped around the outside bottom of the structure where the center support sits.

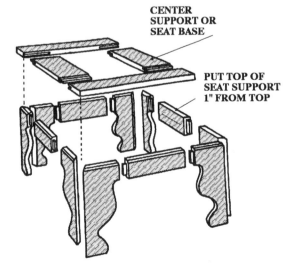

CENTER SUPPORT OR SEAT BASE

PUT TOP OF SEAT SUPPORT 1" FROM TOP

the other side three inches from the top as shown. Allow the assembly to dry overnight.

7. Remove the web clamp, turn the assembly over and drill four holes on each side through the outside of the legs and spacers into the center support. Try to make all of the holes uniform and in line.

Screw the screws into the holes. Glue ½" wood plugs into the holes and sand flush.

8. Using a cove bit and a router, rout the outside top of the footstool assembly. Using a rounding over bit and a router, rout the outside of

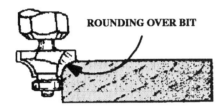

ROUNDING OVER BIT

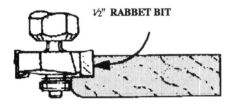

½" RABBET BIT

the legs and leg spacers. Sand the whole assembly thoroughly.

9. Using a walnut-colored Danish oil, stain the project thoroughly. Allow the excess to stay on the wood for about 15 minutes and then wipe it off. Wait 24 hours and do this again.

10. Wrap the fabric around the 2" foam pad and staple it to the underside of the ¼" plywood. Pull the fabric snugly around the foam, tucking the ends so the grain or pattern of the fabric is straight.

11. Using four 1" screws, attach the cusion assembly to the foot stool from the underside corners of the center support.

12. Stand back and pat yourself on the back for a job well done.

NOTES AND CALCULATIONS

Sweetheart Mirror and Change Holder

This project is a snap to make and is quite functional. It not only holds your change, but it also holds ties and belts and other wardrobe items as well. This project will look good in a hallway or bathroom or bedroom wall as well.

MATERIALS

¾ " red oak 8" x 124"
  1 piece 6½ "x 29" top
  1 piece 6¾ " x 29" bottom
  2 pieces 6" x 15½ "sides
  1 piece 4" x 17" tray
  2 pieces 1½ " x 4" tray side trim
  1 piece 1½ "x 18½ " tray front trim
  2 pieces 3" x 3" tray support

HARDWARE AND MISCELLANEOUS

Carpenter's or Titebond glue
7 shaker wood pegs 3"
8 biscuit splines #20
1 mirror 16" x 16" x ⅛ "
4 screws 1½"
2 screws ¾ "
Clear silicone
8 wire brads 1"
Wire strand 60"
1 pint stain sealer

TOOLS REQUIRED

Saber saw
Table or radial arm saw
Drill with ½ " countersink bit
  and ½ " drill bit
Pad sander
Pipe clamps 36"
Router with rounding over bit,
  rabbet bit and a ⅛" slot cutter
Tape measure
Chisel

ONE SQUARE = 1"

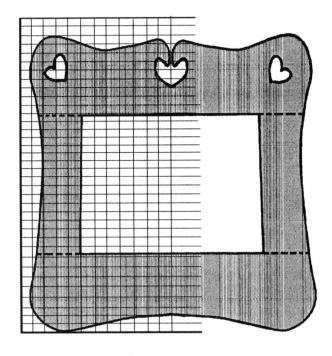

INSTRUCTIONS

1. Copy the wood piece designs for the sides, top and bottom to 1x8 red oak wood stock and cut to size. Drill ½" starter holes for the heart cutouts and cut to shape.

2. Using the router and the ⅛" slot cutter, cut blind slots in the ends of the side boards and top and bottom board.

INCORRECT SETTING

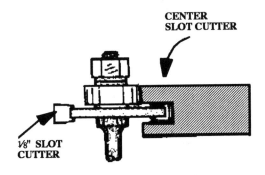

CENTER
SLOT CUTTER

⅛" SLOT
CUTTER

3. Glue the biscuit splines into the slots and clamp the sides, top and bottom boards and allow to set up for at least 6 hours.

4. Measure and cut the pieces for the tray, tray support and edges.

5. Glue and clamp the sides, front and tray.

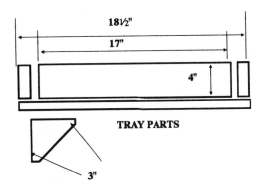

TRAY PARTS

6. After the tray and main mirror wood frame pieces are dry, rout the edges with a rounding over bit. Rout both the tray top and bottom, not the back. Rout the front of the mirror wood frame.

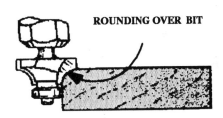

ROUNDING OVER BIT

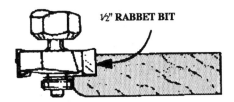

½" RABBET BIT

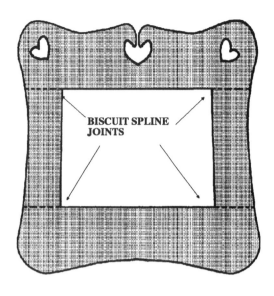

BISCUIT SPLINE JOINTS

10. Carefully place the mirror into the recess in the back of the frame and hold in place with small wire brads and a bead of clear silicone. Be very careful at this juncture not to break the mirror. Allow the silicone to dry before hanging the mirror.

11. Attach a wire across the top back of the assembly, securely twisted to two ¾" wood screws partially screwed into the upper part of the back. Hang the assembly in your place of choice, making certain the hooks or wall retainers will properly support the weight of the project.

Turn the mirror wood frame over and rout the mirror cut out with a ½" rabbet bit to a depth of ½". Using a chisel, square the corners.

7. Drill ½" holes in the positions where you want to put the shaker pegs. Glue and tap the pegs in place.

8. Center and attach the tray and tray supports to the bottom of the mirror frame as shown in the drawing. Use 1½" screws. Predrill the screw holes with a countersink bit.

9. Stain the assembly the color of your choice. I used a dark walnut Danish oil.

12. Stand back, look in the mirror and smile for a job well done.

Combination Magazine Rack and Tissue Dispenser

This project serves two very important functions: It holds magazines and at the same time will hold up to two rolls of toilet tissue. You can make the heart facings as shown here or use ordinary wood dowels instead. In any event, this project is a welcome addition to any bathroom. It also can be used in the kitchen to hold cookbooks and paper towels.

MATERIALS

1x6 white pine 6 linear feet
   2 pieces 5½" x 21" sides
   1 piece 5½" x 14" top back
   1 piece 4½" x 14" bottom board
   2 pieces 1" x 14" top and bottom
    frame

2x4 white pine 8½" long
   9 pieces 1½" x 8½" facings

HARDWARE AND MISCELLANEOUS

1 piece wood dowel 1" x 16"
14 wood screws 1½" drywall type
14 wood plugs ½"
Carpenter's wood glue
1 pint oil stain or paint

TOOLS REQUIRED

Circular saw
Saber saw
Drill with ½" countersink
  and ½" bit
Screwdriver
Router with rounding over
  bit (optional)
Scroll or band saw

INSTRUCTIONS

1. The wood pieces for the sides, front and back are cut from 1x6 lumber. Measure and cut all of these pieces with a circular saw and cut the curves to shape with a saber saw.

2. Draw the shapes for the heart cutouts onto cardboard and cut to shape with scissors. Using these patterns, draw the heart shapes onto the wood sides and back.

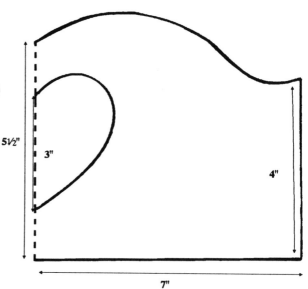

ENLARGE THIS PATTERN AND TRACE
THE LEFT AND RIGHT SIDES

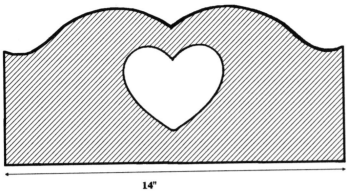

14"

3. Drill a ½" starter hole inside these drawings, and then cut the heart shapes with a saber saw.

4. Draw the shapes for the facings onto the side of the 8½" length 2x4.

5. There are several ways to cut the heart shapes from the 2x4. The most effective way is with a band saw. First cut the heart half to shape and then slice the 2x4 into ¼" strips.

6. Measure and cut the frame piece as one length of 1" x ¾" x 36".

7. Using a circular saw, cut a ¼" x ¼" slot or dado into the center of the frame piece. Cut the frame pieces to length 14".

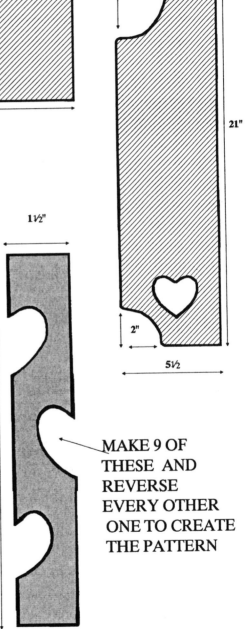

4"

1"

21"

1½"

2"

5½

8½"

MAKE 9 OF THESE AND REVERSE EVERY OTHER ONE TO CREATE THE PATTERN

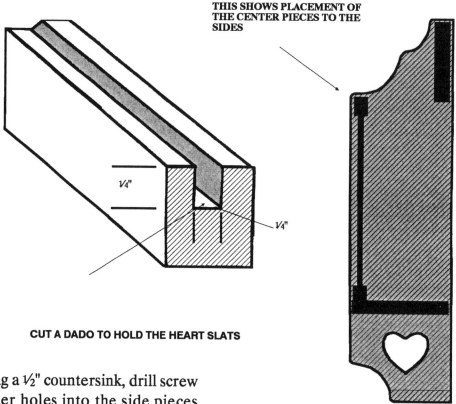

THIS SHOWS PLACEMENT OF THE CENTER PIECES TO THE SIDES

¼"

¼"

CUT A DADO TO HOLD THE HEART SLATS

8. Using a ½" countersink, drill screw starter holes into the side pieces for the top, back and bottom boards.

9. At this juncture, you may opt to rout the front edges of the side boards, the heart shapes and the top of the top board using a router with a rounding over bit. Or you may wish to simply sand the edges to slightly round them. Assemble the above pieces, using screws and glue.

10. Assemble the front frame and facing pieces by inserting the slices into the dado slot in the frame pieces, using glue. Attach this assembly to the front of the assembly from step 9. Use two countersunk screws both in the top and the bottom frame pieces.

11. Glue wood plugs into all of the screw holes and sand flush.

12. Sand the project to remove all rough surfaces.

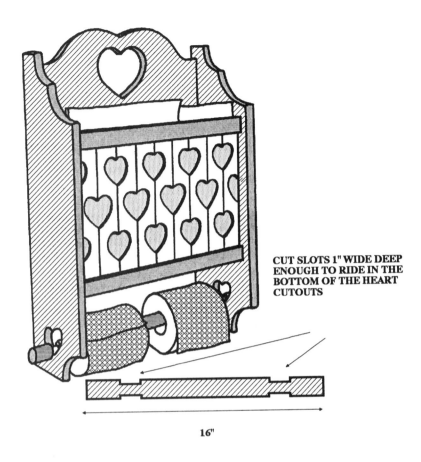

CUT SLOTS 1" WIDE DEEP ENOUGH TO RIDE IN THE BOTTOM OF THE HEART CUTOUTS

16"

13. Cut the wood dowel to length and notch the ends so they fit over the bottom of the heart cutouts.

14. Stain or paint the project the color of your choice. I opted to paint the surface with tole painting designs; you could copy these designs or use stencils to make other designs.

15. Stand back, pat yourself on the back for a job well done and go hang the project in the room of your choice.

NOTES AND CALCULATIONS

Birdhouse Cookie Jar

What a great way to store those fresh homemade cookies everyone likes to gobble down. Who would suspect that a birdhouse might actually be a cookie jar in disguise? This is a fun project to make, and it actually could be a birdhouse if that's what you prefer. Personally though, I prefer the cookie jar.

MATERIALS

1x12 white pine 7 linear feet
   2 pieces 7" x 11¾" bottom front
     and back
   2 pieces 5¾" x 7" sides
   1 piece 10½" x 11¾" base
   2 pieces 8½" x 12" (triangle)
     roof peak
   1 piece 8½" x 9" left roof
   1 piece 8½" x 9¾" right roof
   2 pieces ¾" square 6" long
     corner posts
   2 pieces ¾" x 4½" front posts
   4 pieces ¾" square 3" long
     front rails

   4 pieces ¾" x 2½" long side rails
   1 piece 5¾" x 10½" insert lid
   1 piece ⅛" x ½" x 8½" roof crown

2x10 white pine 12" long
   12 pieces ⅛" x 1" x 3" heart slats
   22 pieces ⅛" x 2" x 8½"
     roof shingles
   1 piece 1½" x 2" x 5" chimney
   1 piece 3½" x 11¾" porch roof

⅛" white acrylic sheet 3 square feet
   2 pieces 7" x 10½" insert front
     and back
   2 pieces 5½" x 7" insert sides
   1 piece 5½" x 10¼" insert bottom

HARDWARE AND MISCELLANEOUS

30 screws 1½" drywall
   variety
30 wood plugs ½"
Silicone glue
Carpenter's or
   Titebond glue
Paint of your choice
1 wood ball 2"
   diameter
Acrylic cement

TOOLS REQUIRED

Circular saw
Drill with ½" bit and
   countersink
Scroll saw or
   band saw
Screwdriver
Router with ½"
   rabbet bit

INSTRUCTIONS

1. Measure and cut all of
   the wood pieces from
   the 1x12 pine wood
   stock.

2. The bottom part of the
   cookie jar is basically a

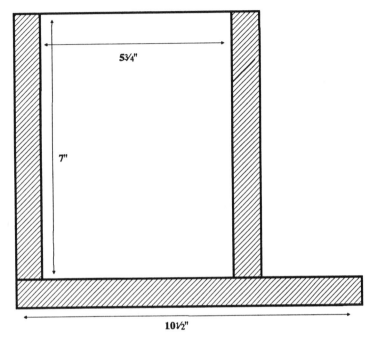

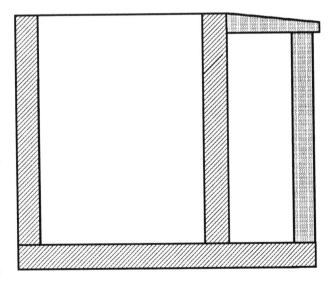

box with four sides and an extended base. Attach the front and back boards to the side boards and then attach the base to this assembly. Use screws that are countersunk, wood plugs to fill the holes and glue. Sand everything flush.

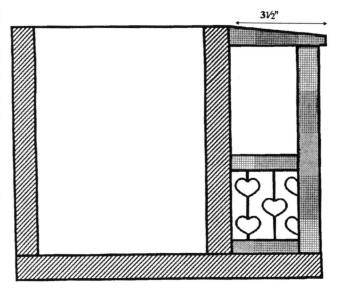

3. The porch roof is a piece of 2" lumber that is cut to fit the length of the front and is tapered to a slant. You can cut this with a circular saw if you're good at making jigs for this purpose. However a band saw is your best bet for cutting the taper.

4. Attach the roof to the upper front using screws driven from the inside of the facing board or front board.

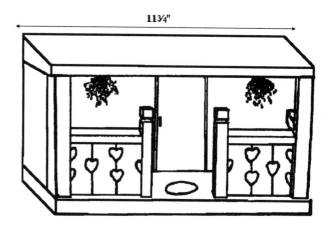

5. Measure and cut the boards forming the roof. The peak boards are essentially triangles to which the roof boards are attached. The roof boards should be first cut

The rails and slats should be glued using clear silicone glue and nailed and glued into position. Experiment with designs of your own such as tulips and other shapes.

to width with a length slightly longer than the two boards needed, sawn at a 45 degree angle in the center and then each board cut to length. The roof boards, when attached, form an L shape that fits over the peak boards. There should be a 1½" overhang at the front. Use screws, glue and wood plugs and sand the . . . well, by now you know the routine.

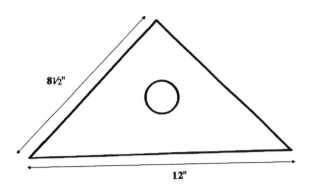

6. The roof shingles and the wood slats forming the heart cutouts on the front porch are cut from the 2" lumber. Let's start with the shingles first. Cut a 2" length of 2x10 against the grain. Next cut 1" deep slots at 1" intervals across the block as shown. You can leave it as is or cut slight angles as shown or round the shapes to obtain the kind of shingle you want. Next cut the shingles to thickness with a band saw or scroll saw.

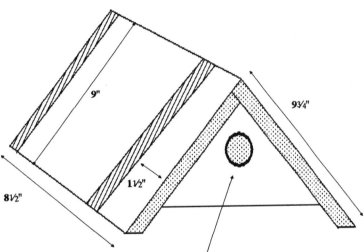

THE OPENING IS MAINLY FOR EFFECT. YOU CAN PAINT IT ON OR DRILL A HOLE THE SIZE YOU WISH

7. Attach the shingles to the roof allowing for a 1" hang over. Use clear silicone glue and no nails. Overlap successive strips of shingles by 1" forming that familiar pattern you see on wood shingle roofs. Cut a small strip of wood to

glue to the very top of the roof, capping the shingles.

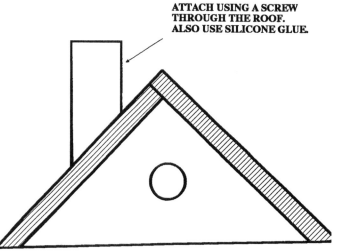

ATTACH USING A SCREW THROUGH THE ROOF. ALSO USE SILICONE GLUE.

8. Measure and cut the chimney from the 2" wood stock and attach to the roof using glue and a wood screw driven from the inside of the roof.

9. Cut lengths of 1" wood stock ¾" square. From this cut the pieces to length that are needed for the front and corner posts and rails. Before cutting the rails to length however, cut a ⅛" slot ¼" deep in the center of one side of the rails. Cut the rails so that you have two pieces about 14" long.

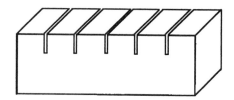

10. Cut a block of wood from the 2" stock that is 1" x 3" x 3". Transfer the designs from the pattern shown and cut the ½ heart shapes. Next slice the slats to a thickness of ⅛".

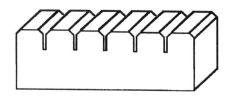

11. Attach the slats into the rails using silicone glue. Allow this assembly to dry thoroughly and then cut the rail slat pieces to size to fit on the sides and front of the porch.

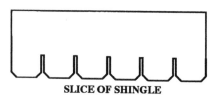

SLICE OF SHINGLE

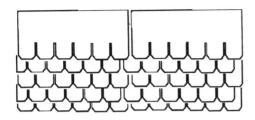

**OVERLAP SHINGLES BY ABOUT 1"
OR AS YOU CHOOSE**

13. Measure and cut the pieces forming the plastic sleeve that fits inside the central chamber. Using masking tape or plastic tape, assemble the structure on top of the bottom acrylic sheet. Apply acrylic cement to the joints so that the structure fuses, forming a solid piece.

14. Insert the assembly from above into the central chamber of the cookie jar.

12. Glue the rails, slats, corner posts and front posts in place using silicone glue and some small wire brads. Allow to dry thoroughly.

15. Measure and cut the lid for the plastic chamber. Rout a ½" rabbet on the edge so the lid fits into and over the plastic insert. Next add a small wood ball as a handle, using a screw and glue.

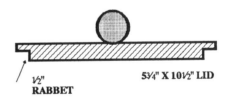

½"
RABBET

5¾" X 10½" LID

16. The final step is your option. I painted mine with a tole painted design. You can stain, paint or do what ever suits your fancy. The big question, however, is how long will it take the kids to figure out where the cookies are?

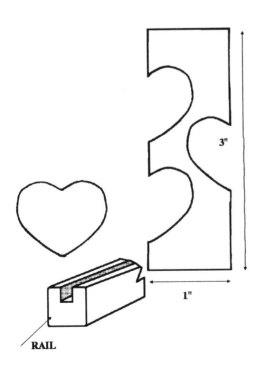

3"

1"

RAIL

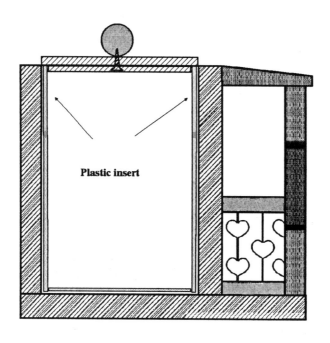

Plastic insert

Checkerboard Game and Coffee Table

This project can be used as a coffee table as well as a game table, plus it's really good looking. This is one of those projects that you need to bone up for since it does take some woodworking skill to get just right. When you're done though, you've got a family heirloom that will be passed down for generations.

MATERIALS

The lumber for this project can be any hardwood you desire, as long as they are contrasting colors. I used pecan and walnut, both nut woods, and very contrasting for the top. Red oak was my next selection for the base. The construction of this project starts with building the base and then the checkerboard top and assembling the two. Last but not least is the required step of putting your feet up after a job well done. At the risk of being criticized for slacking off you can say see, it's right here in print, Baldwin said put your feet up.

1x2 red oak 12 square feet
    2 pieces 18" x 19" legs
    4 pieces 3" x 19" feet
    4 pieces 3" x 6" inner feet
    1 piece 3" x 33" center support
    2 pieces 1" x 19" brace
    2 pieces 2" x 21" end frame
    2 pieces 2" x 37½" side frame
    2 pieces 2" x 22½" end trim
    2 pieces 2" x 39" side trim
    20 pieces 1" x 1" (triangular)
      glue block

1x12 walnut 3 linear feet
    4 pieces 2⅛" x 36"

1x12 pecan 3 linear feet
    4 pieces 2⅛" x 36"

½" plywood 5 board feet
    1 piece 17" x 34" base

HARDWARE AND MISCELLANEOUS

    2 pieces wood dowel ¾" x 3"
    Carpenter's or Titebond glue
    20 wood screws 1½" drywall type
    20 wood plugs oak ½"
    1 pine clear Danish oil

TOOLS REQUIRED

    Table saw
    Saber saw
    Drill with ½" bit and countersink
    Router with chamfering and
      rounding over bit
    Hammer
    Chisel ½"
    Pipe clamps
    Belt sander
    Pad sander

INSTRUCTIONS

1. Measure and cut the 2⅛" wide strips of pecan and walnut.

2. On a flat surface, arrange the pecan and walnut strips alternately

on top of the pipe clamps. Glue up the pieces as shown and wait 24 hours before doing anything with it. Yes, I know that aliphatic resin, which is what carpenter's and Titebond glue comprises, drys in about an hour. However, you are going to be cutting small strips from this assembly later, and if the glue is not properly set, you will have a mess on your hands. So, please make certain the glue is dry before proceeding. While this is going on, start on the base.

soften the appearance of the finished unit and I think adds to its good looks.

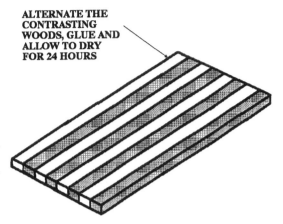

ALTERNATE THE CONTRASTING WOODS, GLUE AND ALLOW TO DRY FOR 24 HOURS

2. Measure and cut the oak pieces forming the base. Drill a starter hole and cut out the opening in the leg for the center support tenon. It is ¾" wide and 2½" high. Use a saber saw for this purpose.

3. The legs that make up the bottoms of the sides are sandwiched between two feet and two inner feet. Assemble each side and fasten all the pieces as shown using countersunk screws and glue and wood plugs for the screw holes. If you wish, rout the legs and feet with a router and a rounding over bit. This tends to

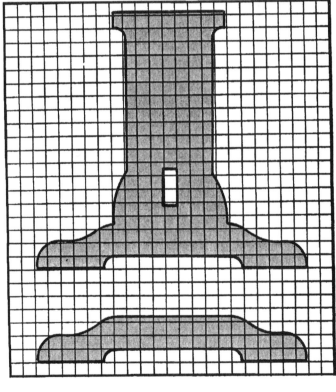

4. Measure and cut the end tenons from the center support. Dry assemble the pieces and carefully mark the location to drill the ¾" hole for the dowel peg as shown. You want the peg to draw the assembly tight so the hole should be a little to the inside of the leg slot. Slightly taper and flatten one side of the dowel rod and tap in place using glue.

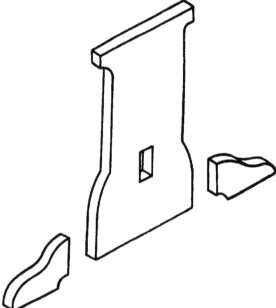

5. The next step is to cut the strips from the by-now-dried wood assembly from step 1. If you're good, you can do this with a circular saw. However, I recommend the use of a table saw with a fine kerf blade. Cut 2⅛" strips from this assembly.

6. Sand off any splinters or rough edges. re-assemble these pieces making up the checker board pattern by flip flopping every other board. Glue and clamp securely and wait 24 hours.

7. Measure and cut the trim and the frame boards. These are mitered on the ends and I suggest that you measure the final size of your assembly from above twice and make adjustments to the sizes stated. This is to make certain you are cutting the boards to fit pro-

THE FEET ARE SANDWICHED AROUND THE LEG

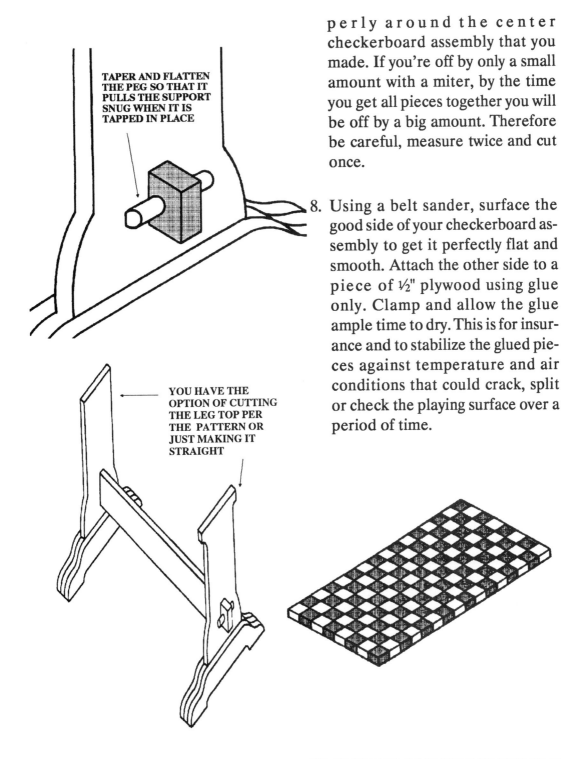

TAPER AND FLATTEN THE PEG SO THAT IT PULLS THE SUPPORT SNUG WHEN IT IS TAPPED IN PLACE

YOU HAVE THE OPTION OF CUTTING THE LEG TOP PER THE PATTERN OR JUST MAKING IT STRAIGHT

perly around the center checkerboard assembly that you made. If you're off by only a small amount with a miter, by the time you get all pieces together you will be off by a big amount. Therefore be careful, measure twice and cut once.

8. Using a belt sander, surface the good side of your checkerboard assembly to get it perfectly flat and smooth. Attach the other side to a piece of ½" plywood using glue only. Clamp and allow the glue ample time to dry. This is for insurance and to stabilize the glued pieces against temperature and air conditions that could crack, split or check the playing surface over a period of time.

9. Attach the trim and frame pieces to the checkerboard center using screws and glue. Do the frame first and then enclose with the trim.

10. Using a router with a chamfering bit, rout the table top and bottom as shown.

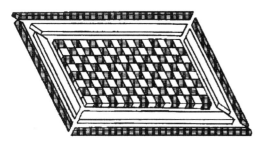

11. Using a pad sander, finish smoothing the surface of the top.

12. Attach small triangular glue blocks at several locations of the side and end trim boards for stability. I suggest two on the ends and three on the sides. Glue to the inside of the trim and the bottom of the plywood.

13. Center and add the brace boards to the top of the legs. Use screws and glue. Position the top on this assembly and attach from underneath.

14. I used three applications of clear Danish oil on the surface, allowing several days between coats. You

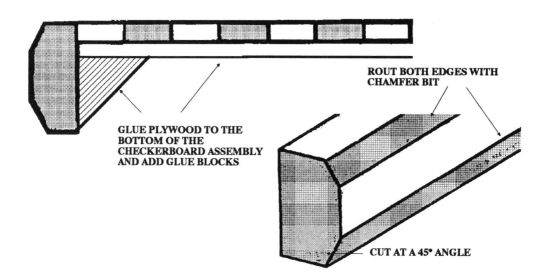

GLUE PLYWOOD TO THE BOTTOM OF THE CHECKERBOARD ASSEMBLY AND ADD GLUE BLOCKS

ROUT BOTH EDGES WITH CHAMFER BIT

CUT AT A 45° ANGLE

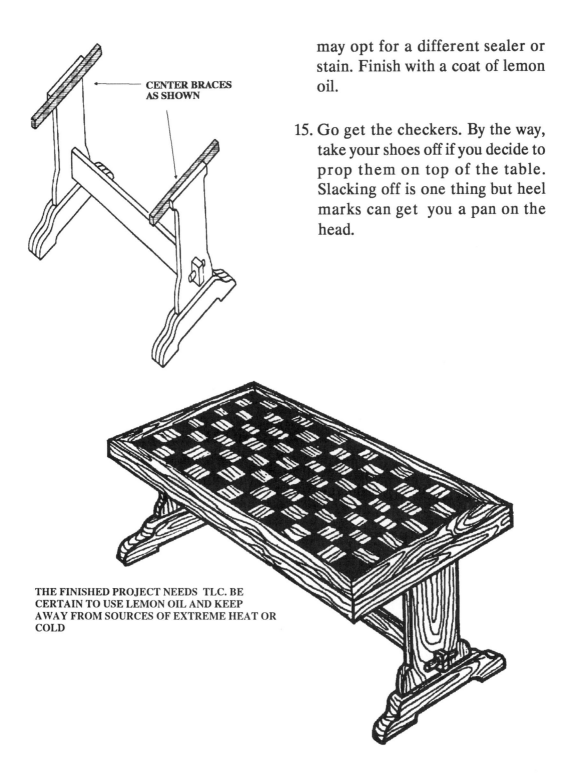

CENTER BRACES
AS SHOWN

may opt for a different sealer or stain. Finish with a coat of lemon oil.

15. Go get the checkers. By the way, take your shoes off if you decide to prop them on top of the table. Slacking off is one thing but heel marks can get you a pan on the head.

THE FINISHED PROJECT NEEDS TLC. BE CERTAIN TO USE LEMON OIL AND KEEP AWAY FROM SOURCES OF EXTREME HEAT OR COLD

NOTES AND CALCULATIONS

Sweetheart Shadow Box

This unique design will brighten up any room it's in. Made from 1" pine boards and tole painted, this project is not only good looking, it is also very functional. Designed to hold knicknacks and odds and ends, it will also hold cups or towels as well.

MATERIALS

¾" pine 8" x 260"
- 2 pieces 7 ½" x 24" sides
- 1 piece 6" x 22 ½" back top
- 1 piece 6 ½" x 22½" back bottom
- 3 pieces 7½" x 22½" shelves
- 1 piece 7½" x 22½" center back
- 1 piece 5" x 22½" center back
- 2 pieces 6" x 6½" doors
- 3 pieces 5" x 7½" middle shelf spacers
- 2 pieces 6½" x 7½" bottom shelf spacers

HARDWARE AND MISCELLANEOUS

- 2 pieces fence mesh ½" squares 5" x 5" door mesh
- 4 hinges 1"
- 36 screws 1½"
- 4 shaker pegs 4"
- 2 small porcelain knobs
- 1 medium bottle carpenter's glue
- 1 pint varnish
- 1 pint stain of your choice
- 36 wood plugs ½"

TOOLS REQUIRED

Saber saw
Drill with ½" countersink bit
¼" and ½" drill bits
Screwdriver
Circular saw
Router with rounding over bit
Pipe clamps

INSTRUCTIONS

1. Using the drawing measurements lay out the various shapes on the the 1x8 lumber. The nominal width of a 1x8 is ¾" x 7½" so the straight cuts are minimal. Measure and cut all wood pieces. Drill a starter hole for all of the heart cutouts with a ½" drill bit. Use a sabre saw to cut the heart shapes to size.

SHADOW BOX TOP

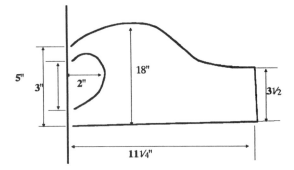

SHADOW BOX BOTTOM

SHADOW BOX SIDE

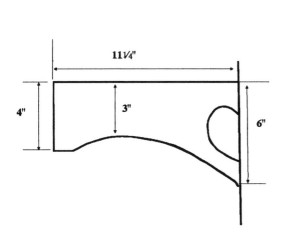

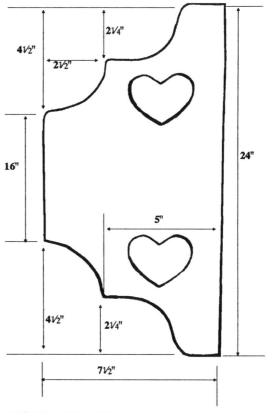

SHADOW BOX BACK

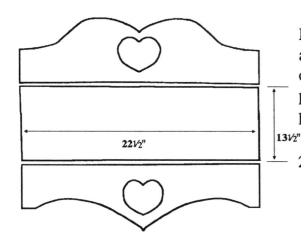

NOTE: The following two drawings are only half a top and half a bottom of the pattern. Be sure to double the pattern size before cutting out the pieces.

2. Using a router with a rounding over bit, rout the facing edge of the shelves and spacers. Rout the facing edge of the sides and the heart cutouts. Rout the front of the door edges and the heart cutout. Rout

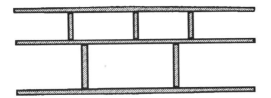

SHELVES

DOOR

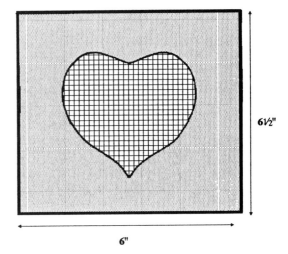

6½"

6"

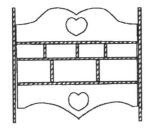

COMPLETE ASSEMBLY

the top edge of the back top and the heart cutout. Rout the bottom

edge of the bottom back board and the heart cutout.

3. Assemble the boards forming the back and glue them together using plain butt joints. Hold in place with pipe clamps.

4. After the back assembly has dried, position the sides and shelves and glue and screw the wood pieces together. Predrill the screw holes with a countersink bit.

5. Attach the screen on the inside of the doors with ½" staples.

Mirrored Candle Sconces

The bright mirrored flame reflected from these candle sconces creates a very warm and romantic feeling. If you are my age, the word homey is used instead of romantic. In any event, they are especially handy when the electricity goes out in a thunderstorm. In fact, you may want to make some of these for every room in the house.

MATERIALS

1x6 red oak 30 linear inches
    1 piece 5" x 18" back
    1 piece 2½" diameter candle
      holder
    1 piece 4" x 5" shelf
    1 piece 3" x 4" bracket

HARDWARE AND MISCELLANEOUS

1 piece mirrored plastic
  ⅛" x 3½" x 8"
2 screws 1½" drywall type
1 screw ¾"
Carpenter's or Titebond glue
1 picture frame hook
Glass mantle 2½" to 3" bottom,
  8" to 9" tall
1 tube silicone caulk
1 pint Danish oil walnut color

TOOLS REQUIRED

Circular saw
Saber saw
Drill with ½" countersink, ¾" and
  ½" bits
Screwdriver
Router with rabbeting, rounding
  over and cove bits
Router pad

INSTRUCTIONS

1. Enlarge the patterns as shown to the sizes listed, using a copying machine with an enlarging capability. The back will exceed the 17" length limit of most copying systems, so two pieces of paper will be needed to enlarge it to its

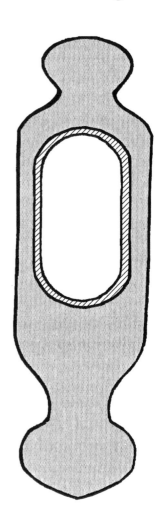

length of 18", or you may opt to keep the length to 17". You can bypass this step if you're good at drawing.

2. Cut your patterns to shape using scissors and trace their outlines onto red oak lumber.

3. Cut the pieces to shape using a circular and sabre saw.

4. Drill a ½" starter hole in the center of the back piece and cut the center part to size. This will house the mirrored plastic.

5. Using a router with a rounding over bit, rout the outside edges of the back, shelf, bracket and candle holder. Use a router pad, something that looks like a rug pad, to hold the smaller pieces. Rout the inside cutout of the back board.

6. Using a router and a cove bit, rout the bottom of the shelf board. This step is optional.

7. Using a router with a rabbeting bit, rout the back of the back board creating a dado ledge in the center cutout to hold the mirrored plastic.

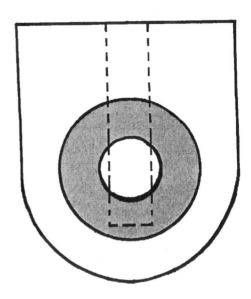

SHELF

ENLARGE THESE PATTERNS TO THE PROPER SIZE USING A COPYING MACHINE

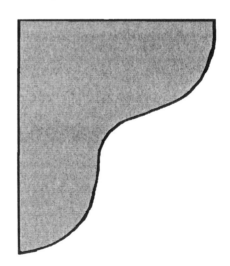

BRACKET

8. Drill a ¾" hole into the center of the candle holder, leaving about a ⅛" base of wood. In other words, don't drill through the piece. Note that some candles have a smaller bottom diameter. I suggest you buy the candles you want to use and measure the bottom diameter and drill the hole the appropriate size.

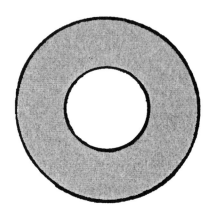

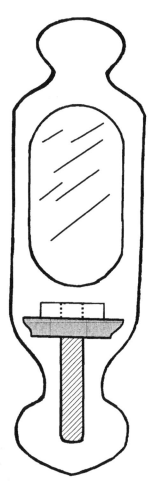

COMPLETED ASSEMBLY

CANDLE HOLDER

9. At this juncture, sand all of the wood pieces to remove any rough edges.

10. Using a countersink drill bit, pre-drill the screw holes in the back, the shelf and the candle holder.

11. Assemble all pieces using screws and glue.

12. Measure and cut the mirrored plastic to fit the recess in the back of the back board. Cut this to shape using great care and a saber saw.

13. Stain the project the color of your choice. I used a walnut colored Danish oil that really makes the oak grain stand out.

14. Remove the protective plastic from the mirrored plastic and inset it into the back cutout. Run a ¼" bead of silicone caulk around the edge of the wood and back of the plastic and allow to dry.

15. Attach a small picture frame hanger on the back. Insert the candle of your choice, add the glass shield or mantle and hang the project on the wall of your own choosing.

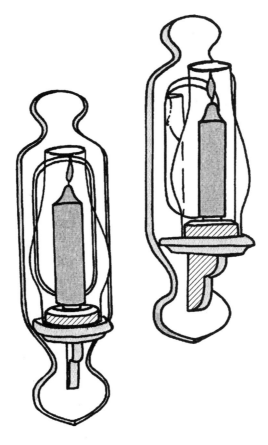

NOTES AND CALCULATIONS

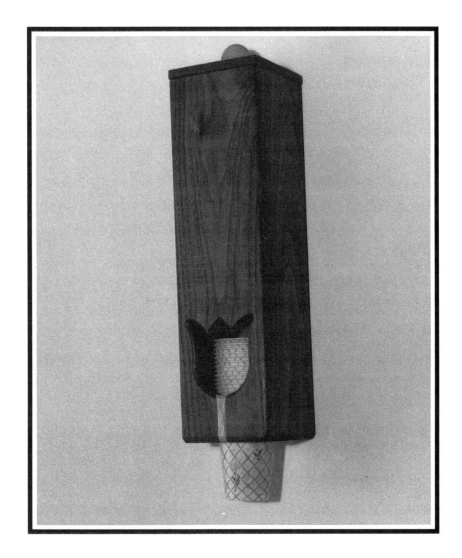

Paper Cup Dispenser

If you have children, this project is a necessity. Paper cups are easier to deal with than dirty cups and glasses. The tulip motif and the inlaid stem look nice, plus I made this from walnut and it really added a touch of class to the kitchen.

MATERIALS

¼" walnut 3 board feet
    2 pieces 4" x 14" front and back
    2 pieces 3½" x 14" sides
    1 piece 4" x 4" lid top
    1 piece 3½" x 3½" inner lid

HARDWARE AND MISCELLANEOUS

1 wood ball 1"
Carpenter's or Titebond glue
1 screw 1½" drywall type
1 piece scrap ¼" wood, ash or oak for stem
1 piece pine ¾" x 3½" square, base
1 pint Danish oil

TOOLS REQUIRED

Circular saw
Clamps
Saber saw or coping saw
Screwdriver
Drill with countersink bit
Router with rounding over bit
Sandpaper

INSTRUCTIONS

1. Measure and cut all of the walnut pieces to size.

2. Cut the tulip and stem design from the front board.

3. Trace the stem design using the board you just cut as the pattern and cut to size. Glue the stem in place clamping the board from the side.

THIS IS A FULL SIZE PATTERN

4. Draw the layout for the base onto a piece of ¾" pine or some other softwood. Using a paper cup as the pattern, draw the circle outline of the top centered on the board. Drill a starter hole and cut the circle to size as indicated, at a slight angle inward, using a saber saw. The whole idea is to allow the rim of the cup to fit into the hole slightly but not fall through. Using a router with a rounding over bit, rout the top edge of the hole. Lift the board and try dropping a cup into the hole. It should take a firm tug or pull to pull the cup through the bottom of the hole. This step is important as the weight of the paper cups may force all of the

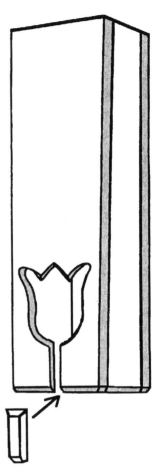

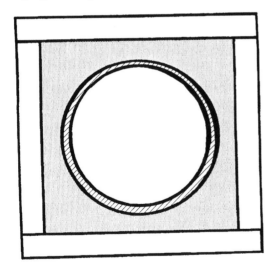

cups to drop to the floor. Cut the board to size.

5. Glue and clamp the front, back, sides and base board and allow to dry overnight.

6. The lid is made up of two pieces of walnut as shown, with a ball on top as the handle. Hold this assembly together with glue and a screw.

7. Stain the project with a clear Danish oil. Drill a small hole at the upper back, angled upward, so that a 2" finishing nail head will fit in it. Decide on your room of choice. Put a 2" finishing nail into the wall and hang the project.

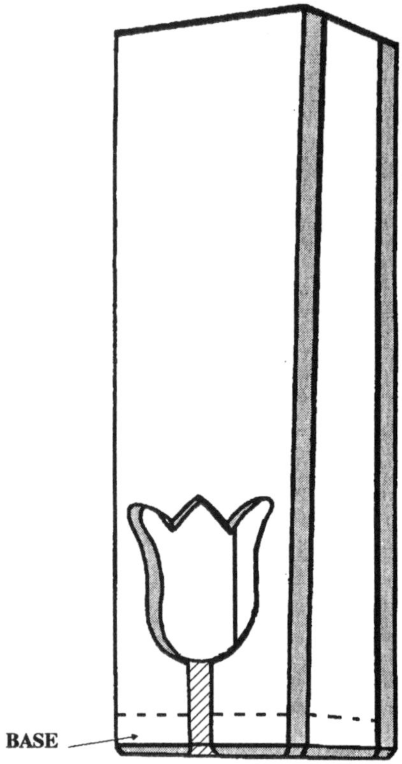

BASE

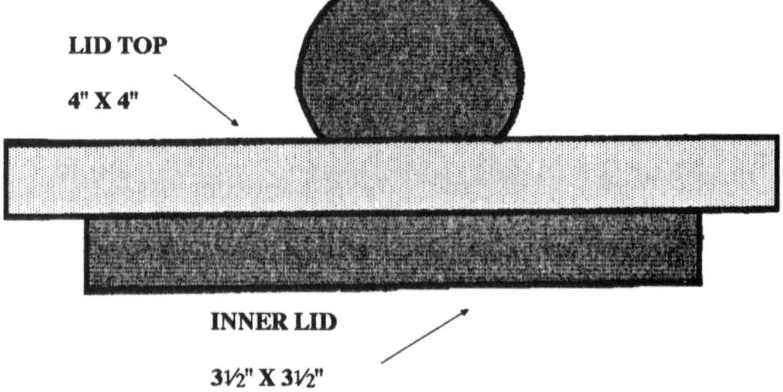

LID TOP

4" X 4"

INNER LID

3½" X 3½"

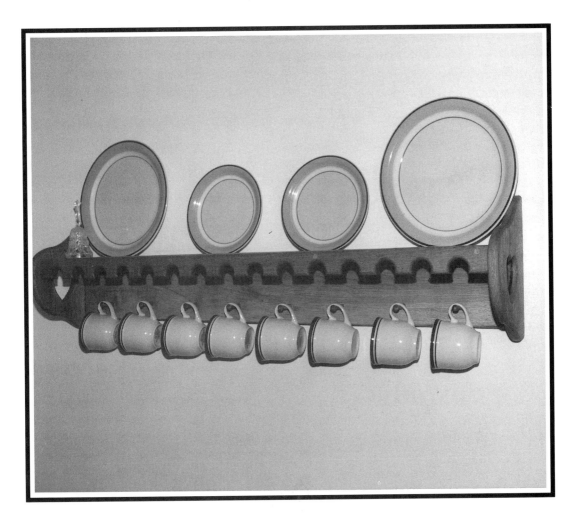

Plate and Cup Rack

This simple structure will add a touch of class to your kitchen or dining room. It's amazingly simple to construct with only four wood pieces. You can use pine or a hardwood. I choose to use red oak and a walnut stain, and the results won lots of praise. You can accomplish the same over an evening or weekend.

MATERIALS

3/4" red oak 8" x 120"
  1 piece 5" x 40" shelf
  1 piece 4" x 40" back
  1 piece 2" x 40" scallop
  2 pieces 5 1/2" x 9" end bracket

HARDWARE AND MISCELLANEOUS

  8 shaker pegs 2" long
  20 screws 1 1/2"
  20 wood plugs 1/2"
  Medium bottle carpenter's or
    Titebond glue
  1 pint Danish oil walnut

TOOLS REQUIRED

  Drill with 1/2" countersink bit and
    1 1/8" spade bit
  Router with rounding over bit and
    1/2" veining bit
  Saber saw
  Circular saw

INSTRUCTIONS

1. Measure and cut the wood pieces. You can enlarge the scale drawings using a copying machine with enlarging or zoom features. The end brackets are 9" long and 5 1/2" wide. The scallop is 2" x 40". I suggest you lay out the holes for the scallop in a straight line with the holes drilled 2 5/8" center to center on a full piece of stock cut to 40". Drill holes to form the scallop pattern with a 1 1/8" drill

BRACKET

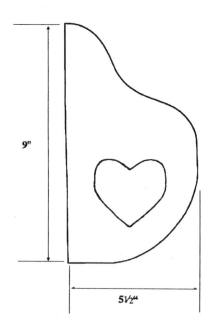

9"

5½"

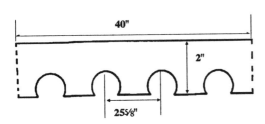

bit and then rip the board to a width of 2" for the pattern as shown.

2. Cut a slot into the top of the shelf board 5/8" wide and 1/4" deep 13/8" from the back of the board and the length of 40". This will form the plate lip or rest. You can do this using a router with a vein-

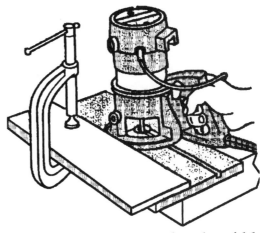

multiple passes, cutting the width of the saw blade until you have reached the 5/8" width. Clamp a wood fence to guide the router or saw.

3. Rout the scallop board with a rounding over bit. Be careful to not rout the ends of the board. Rout the front edge of the end bracket on both sides, including the edges of the heart cutout.

4. Assemble the structure as shown using screws and glue. Predrill the screw holes with a countersink and fill the holes with wood plugs after the screws are firmly attached. The scallop board is attached to the shelf board, flush with the top surface. Use four screws evenly placed for this purpose. The back of the end brackets should be even with the back of the back board. Use two screws into the shelf and

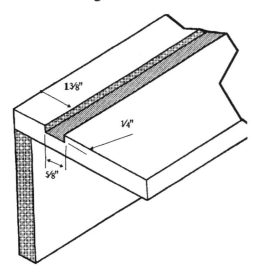

ing bit or with a circular saw and

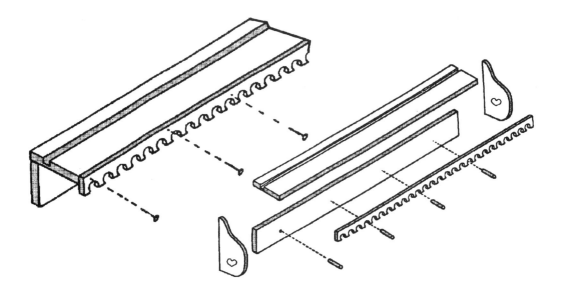

two into the back board through the side of the end bracket.

5. Drill 8 holes into the bottom of the back board for the shaker pegs. You may opt to substitute wood dowels for this purpose. If you use wood dowels, the dowels should have a slight upward tilt so the cups will not slide off.

6. Stain or paint the project the color of your choice.

7. Attach to a wall using molly bolts or toggle bolts large enough to support the weight that you intend for it to hold.

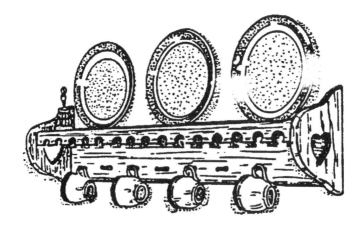

Teddy Bear Settle/Toy Chest

This is a project for that special little person in your life. This is a combination settle that is full size and will seat at least one, if not two, adults. It has a seat/lid combination that lifts and conceals a storage area. The teddy bear cutouts are a cute little accent that are very easy to make.

MATERIALS

1x18 white pine splined stock
    20 linear feet
    1 piece 16" x 34" bottom front
    1 piece 15¾" x 34" floor
    1 piece 17" x 34" lower back
    1 piece 15" x 30¼" seat/lid
    2 pieces 18" x 34" cut to shape
      sides
    2 pieces 1¾" x 17½" seat sides
    1 piece 2⅛" x 30¼" seat back
    2 pieces 1¾" x 8½" upper back
      assembly sides
    1 piece 3" x 34" upper back
      assembly top board
    1 piece 4⅞" x 34" upper back
      assembly bottom board
    2 pieces ¾" x ¾" x 34" floor support
    2 pieces ¾" x ¾" x 12" floor support

2x4 white pine 2 linear feet
    20 pieces ⅛" x 1½" x 9" teddy bear
      strips

HARDWARE AND MISCELLANEOUS

Carpenter's or Titebond glue
2 hinges, brass 3"
40 wood screws 1 ½" drywall type
40 wood plugs ½" pine
1 pint stain or paint of your choice

TOOLS REQUIRED

Drill with ½" countersink and bit
Scroll saw or band saw with
  narrow blade
Saber saw
Sander, pad or belt
Pipe clamps
Router with a rounding over bit
Circular saw or table saw

INSTRUCTIONS

1. Measure and cut all of the wood pieces to size.

2. Using the full size teddy bear pattern provided, draw the design on the upper part of the sides as shown in the illustration. Predrill a starter hole and cut to shape using a saber saw.

3. Using a router with a rounding over bit, rout the sides on both sides, including the area of the teddy bear cutout.

4. The teddy bear strips are cut from a 2x4. Draw the designs on the edge or side of a 9" length of 2x4. Cut the designs using a band saw or scroll saw. Next cut ⅛" slices from the 2x4.

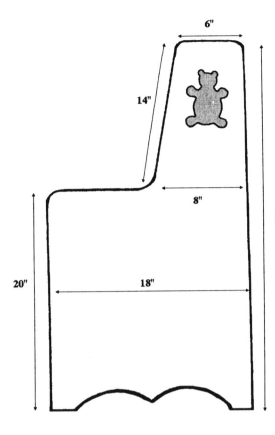

and clamp the pieces until the glue is dried.

7. Assemble the settle by attaching the sides to the front, lower back and upper back assembly. Use screws and glue, countersink the screws. Glue wood plugs into the screw holes and sand flush.

8. Attach the floor support boards to the inner sides, front and back, about 4" from the bottom. Attach

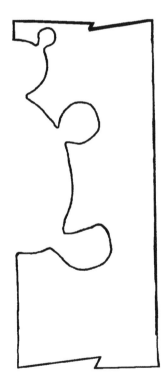

Sand the finished pieces.

5. Cut a 1/8" dado in the center of the edges of the upper back side, top and bottom boards. Make this cut 1/4" deep.

6. Assemble the teddy bear back by flip flopping every other teddy bear strip. Place these into the dado slots cut into the side, top and bottom boards forming the upper back assembly. Use glue

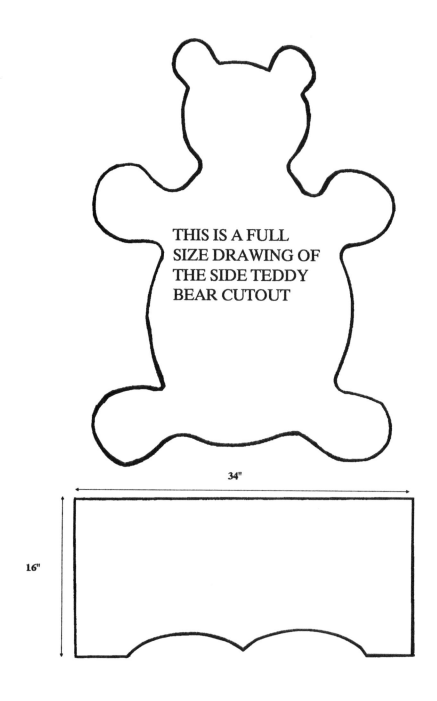

THIS IS A FULL
SIZE DRAWING OF
THE SIDE TEDDY
BEAR CUTOUT

34"

16"

FRONT BOTTOM OF TOY CHEST

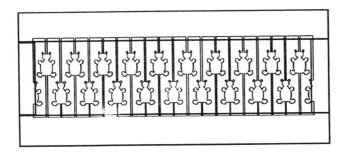

TEDDY BEAR BACK ASSEMBLY

1½"

9"

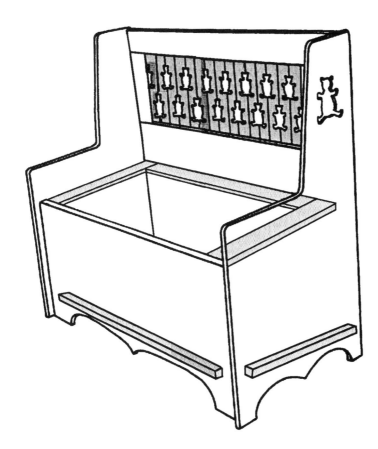

ATTACH THE FLOOR AND SEAT SUPPORTS AS SHOWN

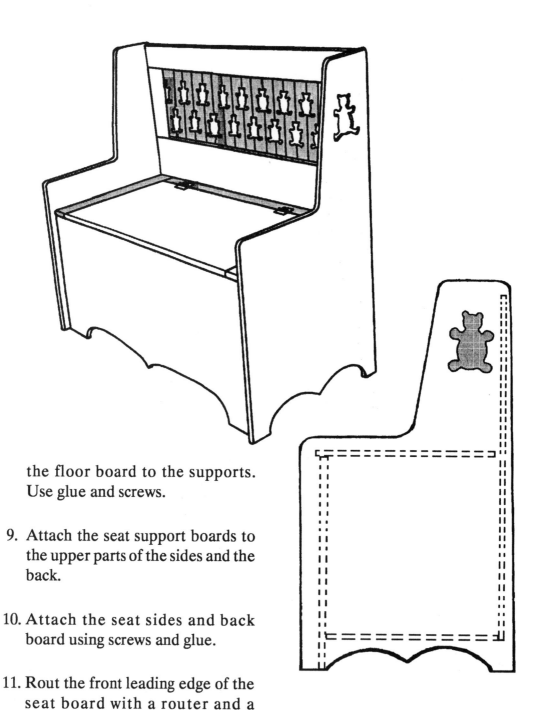

the floor board to the supports.
Use glue and screws.

9. Attach the seat support boards to
the upper parts of the sides and the
back.

10. Attach the seat sides and back
board using screws and glue.

11. Rout the front leading edge of the
seat board with a router and a
rounding over bit. Attach the
seat/lid using hinges.

NOTE PLACEMENT OF BOARDS

12. Paint or stain the project the color of your choice.

The finished project is a perfect gift for that special child in your life. But please put a plywood backing on the area of the little bear cutouts if this is used for extremly small children because the small shapes could catch and hurt little fingers.

THE FINISHED PROJECT

NOTES AND CALCULATIONS

Curved Back Chairs and Rockers

These are very strong chairs that incorporate many of the features of Early American furniture. They are made from red oak, featuring interlocking mortise and tenon joints and should last for several generations. The seats are upholstered with foam and a fabric that reflects a warm country aura. These projects are certain to warm up every room you put them in.

MATERIALS

The basic chair is the same for the armchair and rocker. This material list is for one chair plus the additional materials needed for the armchair and rocker.

2" red oak surfaced 1½" x 10" x 48"
    2 pieces 1½" x 2" x 45" back leg
    2 pieces 1½" x 1½" x 17" front leg
    2 pieces 1½" x 2½" x 17½" seat frame side
    1 piece 1½" x 2½" x 18½" seat frame front
    1 piece 1½" x 2½" x 16½ " seat frame back

2 pieces 1½" x 1¾" x 10¾" armchair post
10 pieces ¼" x 1½" x 38" rocker laminates

3/4" red oak surfaced ¾" x 8" x 72"
    2 pieces 2" x 15½" side rails
    1 piece 2" x 16⅝" front rail
    1 piece 2" x 14½" back rail
    2 pieces 1¼" x 15⅛" seat brace sides
    1 piece 1¼" x 16" seat brace front
    1 piece 1¼" x 14 " seat brace back
    2 pieces 4¾" x 17" armrests

¼" green red oak 4" x 48"
   3 pieces ¼ " x 3¾" x 15¼" chair
   back slats

¼" plywood
   1 piece 16" x 15⅛" x 14" seat

¾" pine or the equivalent 8" x 16 feet
   4 pieces 8" x 48" rocker bending
   frame

HARDWARE AND MISCELLANEOUS

4 wood plugs ½" oak (armchair)
Carpenter's or Titebond glue
12 screws 1½"
1 piece foam rubber 2" x 16"
1 piece upholstery fabric 24" x 24"
1 quart Danish oil walnut

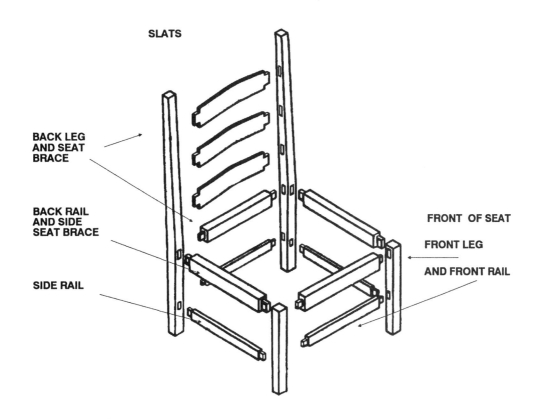

SLATS

BACK LEG
AND SEAT
BRACE

BACK RAIL
AND SIDE
SEAT BRACE

SIDE RAIL

FRONT OF SEAT

FRONT LEG

AND FRONT RAIL

TOOLS REQUIRED

Radial arm saw or table saw
Band saw
Screwdriver
Drill with countersink bit
and ½" bit (optional)
Chisel ½"
Saber saw
Pad sander and belt sander
Flap wheel sander
Drill press with mortising
  chisel
Stapler and ¼" staples

INSTRUCTIONS

The basic chair frame is the same for the chair, the rocker and the armchair. Almost every joint in this chair is a mortise and tenon joint. You can opt to cut the joints using hand-held tools or by using a band saw and drill press with a mortising chisel set up. Or you can use a router with a mortise jig. You can also modify these plans and substitute the mortise and tenon with wood dowels or biscuit splines.

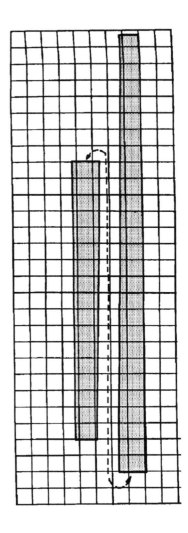

1 SQUARE = 1 INCH

1. A scale drawing is provided for the back legs. Enlarge the drawing and cut the two back legs. I suggest you cut a 2" strip of the 2" stock 45" long and then taper the top and bottom as shown.

2. Using the drawing that illustrates the mortise positions, mark the positions and outline with a pencil starting at the bottom of the rung. Cut the mortises using a drill press with a mortising chisel

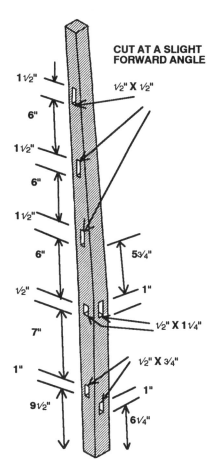

CUT AT A SLIGHT
FORWARD ANGLE

1½"

6"

1½"

6"

1½"

6"

½"

7"

1"

9½"

½" X ½"

5¾"

1"

½" X 1¼"

½" X ¾"

1"

6¼"

or by hand using a drill and ½" bit to drill to the depth of the mortise and a ½" chisel to cut out the corners. Remember that you are making mirror images. The mortises for the slats should angle toward the front of the back leg.

3. Measure and cut the front legs from the 2" red oak stock. Taper the legs so that the top part is 1½"

square and the bottom is 1¼" square. Cut the mortises, again remembering that you are making mirror images.

4. Measure and cut the chair slats. I used green red oak and bent them into a makeshift frame using 1" wood dowels as spacers. I did this during the winter months and sat the assembly next to the

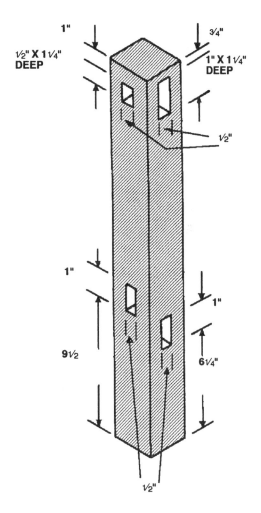

1"

½" X 1¼"
DEEP

¾"

1" X 1¼"
DEEP

½"

1"

9½

1"

6¼"

½"

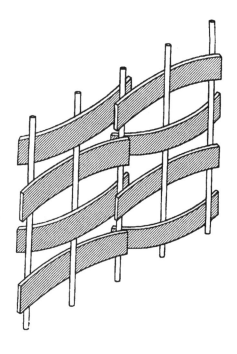

flap wheel sander, slightly rounding all edges.

6. Measure and cut the four rails. At the end of each, cut a ½" x 1" x ¾" tenon. Cut the angles in the ends as shown in the seat assembly top view.

7. Measure and cut the chair side frame pieces as follows. The side frame pieces join the front and back legs with interlocking mortise and tenon joints. They are cut at a slight angle as shown in the overview of the seat assembly. This is a bit of a tricky process and is likely to leave you frustrated if you don't take it

fireplace for a month until the wood dried and retained the bend that I wanted. You can opt to steam the wood or cut the shape using larger stock although the results may not be desirable. I cut the stock ¼" larger than the final size the plans call for.

5. Cut the dried wood slats to size and cut the tulip design in the top slat centered. At this juncture I suggest you sand the slats using a

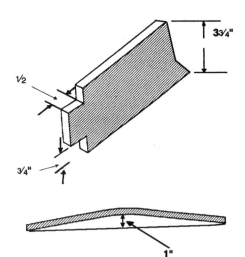

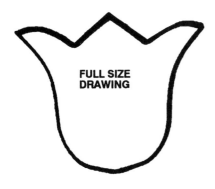

FULL SIZE DRAWING

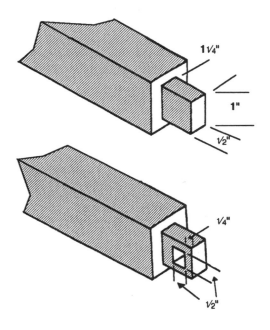

slow, proceeding with caution as you measure and cut each tenon at the right angle. Cut a straight tenon ½" x 1¼" x 1" at each end. Cut a ½" x ½" mortise through each tenon ¼" from the end. This will serve as the lock mortise for the ends of the front and end frame piece tenons you will cut next.

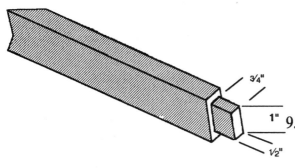

8. Measure and cut the front and back frame pieces. Cut a ½" x ½" x 1¼" tenon at each end. Slip the tenons into the side mortises to see if you have a snug fit. At this juncture you may have to sand the ends to obtain the proper fit. Remember the idea is to have a snug interlocking joint. If you goof and have too much slack, a mixture of sawdust and glue can make up the differences at the assembly time.

9. At this juncture you find out how good your eyesight was as we begin the chair assembly process. I suggest a dry assembly first to make certain everything fits

correctly. First glue and assemble each side assembly by attaching the side frame and rail into the front and back leg piece. Next add the back slats, rail, frame and the front frame and rail into one side. Now attach the other side to these pieces gluing all joints. Clamp the entire assembly and allow it to dry overnight. I know the glue manufacturer says 2 to 3 hours but overnight is better insurance.

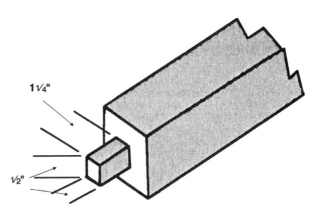

1¼"

½"

a lock joint for each joint in the chair. Sand the dowel flush with the wood surface.

10. This next step is optional. I drilled a ⅛" hole into the center of each tenon joint through the chair legs and inserted a piece of ⅛" wood dowel with glue to form

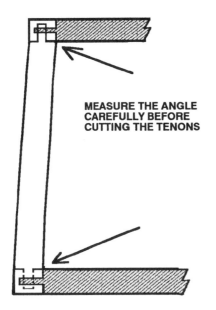

MEASURE THE ANGLE
CAREFULLY BEFORE
CUTTING THE TENONS

11. Using the seat inner frame as a pattern, draw the shape onto the ¼" plywood and hold aside. Measure and cut the seat brace pieces. Center and drill two countersink holes through the inside of each piece and attach it to the inside of the seat frame as shown, allowing a ¼" lip in which the seat assembly will fit. If you're happy with the chair version go to step No. 19.

12. For the armchair version I added a post cut from the 2" stock and an armrest cut from ¾" stock. Measure and cut these pieces to size.

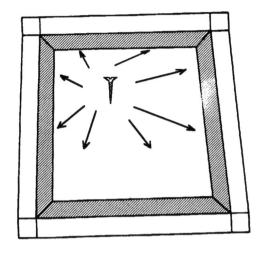

SEAT TOP VIEW

1 SQUARE = 1 INCH

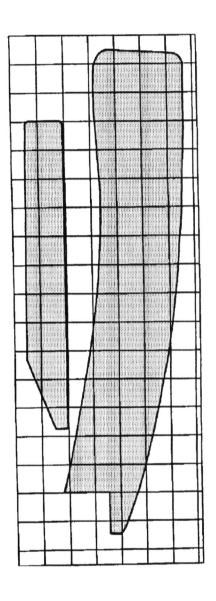

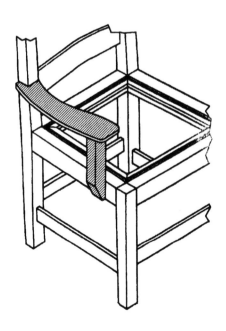

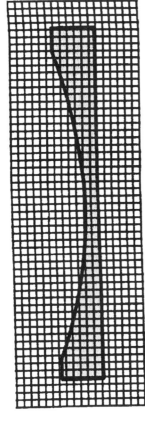

1 SQUARE = 1 INCH

13. Drill two countersink holes in the tapered end of the post 1" from the bottom. Attach it to the chair using glue and screws 3½" from the front of the chair. Attach the armrest to the back leg and post through countersunk holes, using one screw at the back and one down through the post along with glue. Glue wood plugs into the holes and sand flush.

14. For the rocker version you need to cut the rockers and form the bend. To do that make a bending frame by cutting three of the 8" x 48" pine boards as shown. The curve that I used was the arc of a circle with a radius of 5 feet. Or, putting it a different way, I bent the laminates that form the rocker by about 3½".

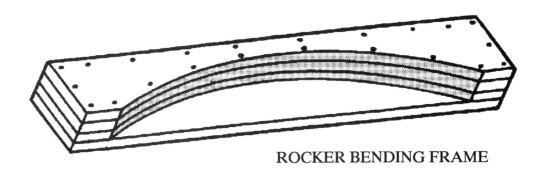

ROCKER BENDING FRAME

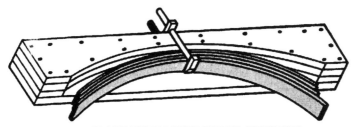

CLAMP THE ROCKER PIECES SECURELY
STARTING AT THE MIDDLE AND WORKING
TOWARDS THE ENDS

15. Stack the boards for the bending frame on top of the uncut board and nail them together. Cover the frame with waxed paper to prevent the rocker assembly from sticking to the frame. Take five of the rocker laminates and cover them with a thin coat of glue. Next place the laminates in the bending frame and bend them to shape using a bar clamp. Use a hammer to tap the edges of the laminates to keep them flat and even. Add clamps at both ends and add two more between the center clamp and the end clamps. Allow this to dry overnight. Make a second rocker.

16. Trim the rockers to about 34". Sand the rockers using a belt sander curving the tips or ends as shown. Using a flap sander, slightly round the edges of the rockers.

17. Place the chair on its side and place the rocker on the front and back legs with the front of the rocker 3" from the front of the front leg. Make certain that the bottom of the rocker and the bottom of the legs are flush. Mark the curve of the rocker on the legs and cut the leg bottoms to shape using a saber saw.

ROUTING THE EDGES OF THE ROCKER WITH A
ROUTER AND A ROUNDING OVER BIT IS THE
FASTEST WAY TO SMOOTH THE EDGES

18. Test the rocking action and make certain it is even and each side is in sync. Use a rasp or sanding paper to make certain the ends of the chair fit flat on the top of the rocker. Mark the leg rocker position and attach the rockers to the bottom of the legs with a screw and glue through a countersunk hole in the bottom of the rocker.

19. Go over the whole chair with a flap wheel sander inserted in a handheld drill.

20. Stain the project using a walnut colored Danish oil stain. Allow this to dry 24 hours and repeat the process.

21. Using the ¼" plywood from step 11 as a pattern, mark the form onto the 2" foam rubber. Cut the foam rubber to size with scissors. Place the foam rubber on the plywood and wrap the assembly with the upholstery material of your choice. Pull the fabric tight, even and smooth, stapling it in place on the underside of the plywood using ¼" staples.

22. Stand back, pat yourself on the back and go find a place to put your new furniture.

Corner Shelves

These shelves are the perfect answer for that hard-to-fill corner of your house. Easy weekend projects that almost give the illusion of a corner hutch for a lot less money. These are good-looking projects sure to please the whole family.

MATERIALS

1x6 white pine 19 linear feet

(Note: all facing boards cut 5" wide,
    back boards 4 ½" wide)

Small shelf
    1 piece 24" facing board
    1 piece 16¼" right back board
    1 piece 15½" left back board

Medium shelf
    1 piece 30" facing board
    1 piece 20" right back board
    1 piece 19¼" left back board

Large shelf
    1 piece 36" facing board
    1 piece 24¼" right back board
    1 piece 23½" left back board

½" plywood 6 board feet
    1 piece 24½" by 34½" large shelf
    1 piece 20½" by 29" medium shelf
    1 piece 19" x 23" small shelf

HARDWARE AND MISCELLANEOUS

18 wood screws 1½" drywall type
30 or so wire brads 1"
Carpenter's or Titebond glue
Wood filler
1 pint paint or stain

TOOLS REQUIRED

Circular saw
Saber saw
Drill with countersink and ½"
    bits
Hammer and nail set
Screwdriver
Router with rounding over and
    rabbet bits
Sander pad or belt

INSTRUCTIONS

1. Rip the 1x6 material to a width of
   5" and then proceed to cut off the
   individual pieces as listed above.
   Remember that the back boards
   must be cut at a 45-degree miter in
   order to be flush with the back of
   the facing boards when assembled.

2. Using a saber saw, cut the shapes
   shown for the three facing boards.
   The curves loop in an arc of about

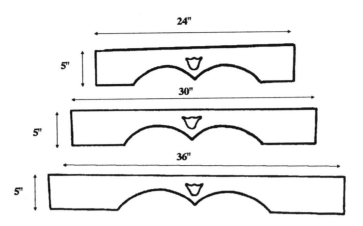

MAKE THREE FACINGS THE SIZE SHOWN

2" from the bottom of the board's edge. I suggest you draw one side, cut the piece and then use it as the pattern for the other side. Drill a ½" starter hole and then cut the tulip shape in the center of each facing board as shown.

3. Measure and cut the plywood pieces to size. You are essentially cutting triangles with two sides of equal length and a wider base.

4. Assemble the back boards, forming a triangle. Use screws and glue. Attach the plywood pieces so that they are flush with the sides and with a ½" lip at the front. Countersink the nails.

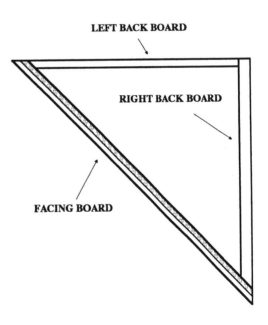

EACH SHELF CONSISTS OF THREE BOARDS PLUS A PLYWOOD INSERT

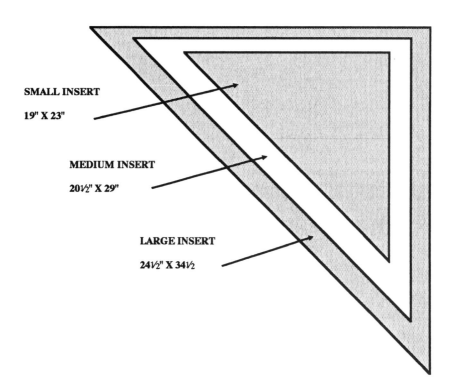

SMALL INSERT

19" X 23"

MEDIUM INSERT

20½" X 29"

LARGE INSERT

24½" X 34½

THE PLYWOOD INSERTS ARE THREE TRIANGLES

5. Using a router with a rabbet bit, rout a ½" by ½" dado in the back of the facing boards.

CUT A ½" x ½" DADO TO RECEIVE THE PLYWOOD INSERT. CUT A 45 DEGREE MITER IN BOTH ENDS OF THE FACING BOARDS AND THE FRONT END OF THE LEFT AND RIGHT BACK BOARDS.

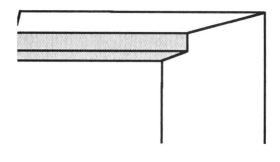

6. Attach the assembly from step 4 and the facing boards. Use glue, nails countersunk through the plywood, and screws from the sides of the back boards into the back of the facing boards, pulling the facing boards snug against the plywood and back boards.

7. Fill the nail holes with wood filler and sand the rough spots.

8. Using a router with a rounding over bit, rout the top and bottom edges of the facing boards as well as the tulip cutout.

9. Stain or paint the finished projects the color of your choice.

10. Attach the shelves to the corner of your choice, using ¼" toggle bolts or other fasteners designed to hold

FULL SIZE PATTERN

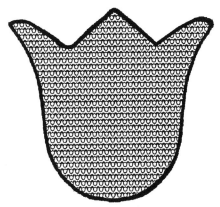

a lot of weight. I suggest you use at least four fasteners for each shelf.

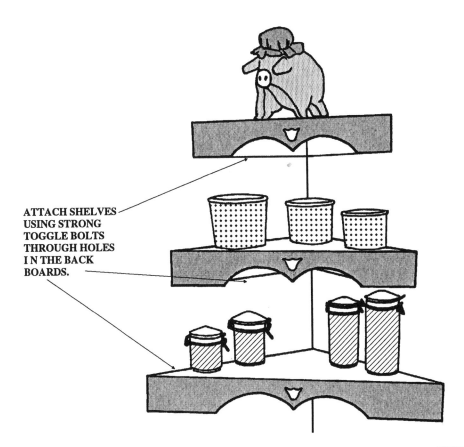

ATTACH SHELVES USING STRONG TOGGLE BOLTS THROUGH HOLES I N THE BACK BOARDS.

NOTES AND CALCULATIONS:

Child's Rocker/Doll Cradle Combo

This project is designed to delight that special little person in your life. Designed as a doll cradle as well as a rocker for small children, this project can also house flowers at the front door. If you wish, a larger model could also be made for Mom.

MATERIALS

¾" pine or spruce 11½" x 14'
- 1 piece 36" long seat/cradle base
- 2 pieces 2 ¾" x 11 ¼" armrests
- 2 pieces 6" x 13 ½" backrest
- 2 pieces 1" x 6" backrest supports
- 2 pieces 10 ½" x 12" rockers
- 2 pieces 10" x 11 ¾" rocker supports
- 1 piece 10 ¼" x 11 ¾" cradle headboard
- 1 piece 5 ¼" x 11 ¾" cradle footboard
- 2 pieces 3½" x 18" cradle sides
- 1 piece 1" x 16" back/armrest support

2x4 pine or spruce
- 2 pieces 2 ¾" long armrest supports

HARDWARE AND MISCELLANEOUS

- 24 screws 1 ½"
- 24 wood plugs ½"
- Carpenter's or Titebond glue
- Paint or stain of your choice

TOOLS REQUIRED

Saber saw
Circular saw
Router with rounding over bit
Screwdriver
Sandpaper
Pipe clamps
Drill with ½" countersink and ½" bit

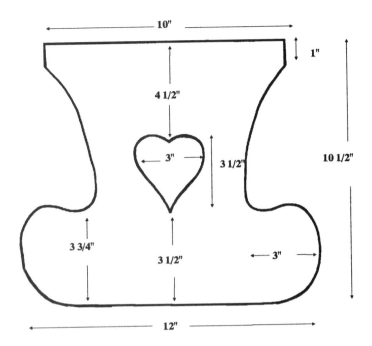

10"

1"

4 1/2"

3"

3 1/2"

10 1/2"

3 3/4"

3 1/2"

3"

12"

**CUT THE ROCKER BOTTOM SO IT IS SLIGHTLY
ROUNDED, ALMOST FLAT. YOU WANT IT TO
ROCK BUT NOT TIP OVER WITH A YOUNGSTER.**

INSTRUCTIONS

1. Enlarge the drawings
   and trace onto 1x12
   wood stock.

2. Cut all pieces to size
   using a circular saw and
   saber saw. The bottom
   of the cradle sides and
   the back pieces should
   be cut at a 20 degree
   angle.

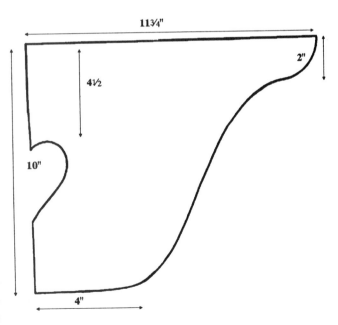

11¾"

2"

4½

10"

4"

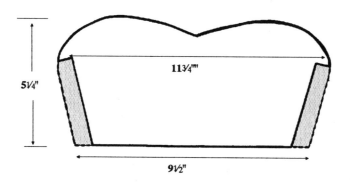

CRADLE FOOT

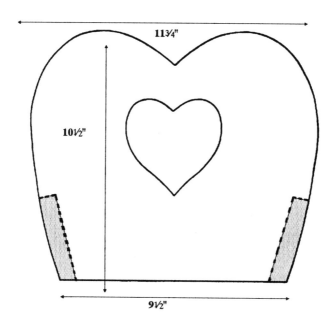

CRADLE HEAD

3. Drill a ½" starter hole and cut out the heart shapes in the rocker and headboard boards.

4. Rout the outside of the rockers and the heart cutout as well as the curved edge of the rocker supports using a router with a rounding over bit.

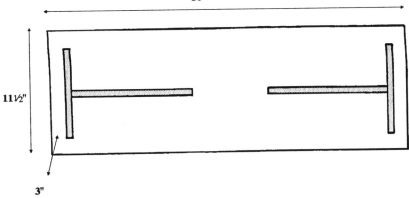

PLACEMENT OF ROCKERS AND BRACES

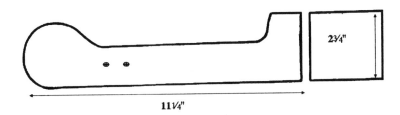

ARMREST AND SUPPORT

5. Rout the edges of the cradle base with a router and a rounding over bit.

6. Attach the rockers and the rocker supports to the bottom of the cradle base. Use screws and glue and pre-drill the screw holes with a countersink.

7. The rocker back consists of two boards. Glue and clamp them and attach the back support boards as shown. Make certain the bottom support will not interfere with the placement of the back support. Allow the assembly to dry thoroughly.

8. Rout the curved part of the cradle headboard, footboard and the top of the side boards using a router with a rounding over bit.

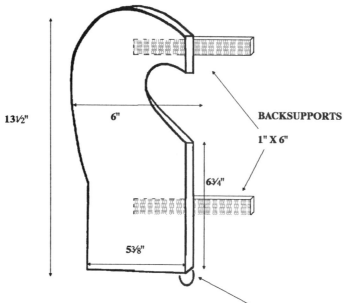

13½"   6"   **BACKSUPPORTS**

1" X 6"

6¾"

5⅜"

BACK—MAKE A MIRROR IMAGE. CUT BOTTOM AT 20 DEGREES

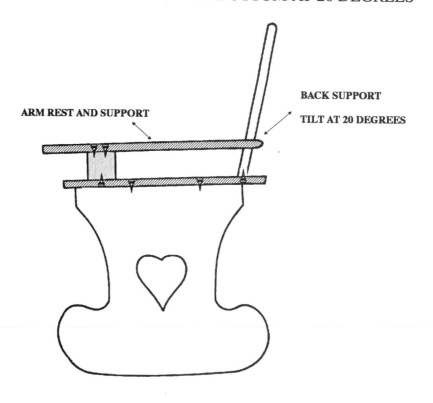

ARM REST AND SUPPORT

BACK SUPPORT

TILT AT 20 DEGREES

9. Attach the cradle headboard and footboard to the side boards using a countersink, screws and glue. Allow the assembly to dry thoroughly.

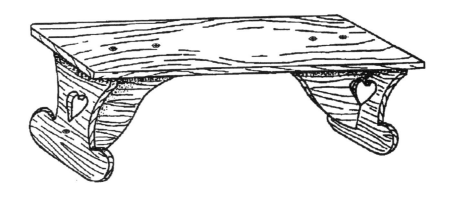

CRADLE AND ROCKER BASE

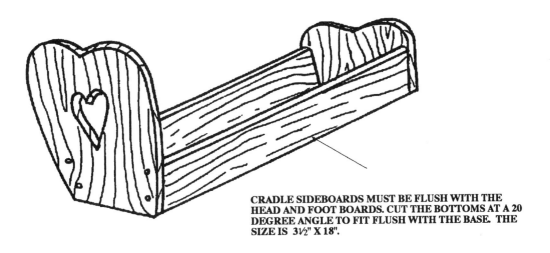

CRADLE SIDEBOARDS MUST BE FLUSH WITH THE HEAD AND FOOT BOARDS. CUT THE BOTTOMS AT A 20 DEGREE ANGLE TO FIT FLUSH WITH THE BASE. THE SIZE IS 3½" X 18".

CRADLE SUBASSEMBLY

10. Rout the sides and front of the arm rests with a router and a rounding over bit. Do not rout the back part that fits against the back support.

11. Attach the arm rests and back support to the rocker back. The back support should be approximately 2 ¾" from the bottom edge of the back. Attach this assembly to the cradle/rocker base and the arm rest supports using glue, screws and a countersink.

12. Position and attach the cradle assembly to the cradle/rocker base using glue, screws and a countersink.

13. Glue wood plugs into the screw holes and sand flush.

14. Paint or stain the project the color of your choice. Remember to use a non-toxic paint.

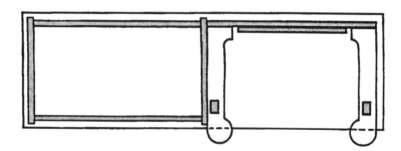

PLACEMENT OF CRADLE AND ARM RESTS

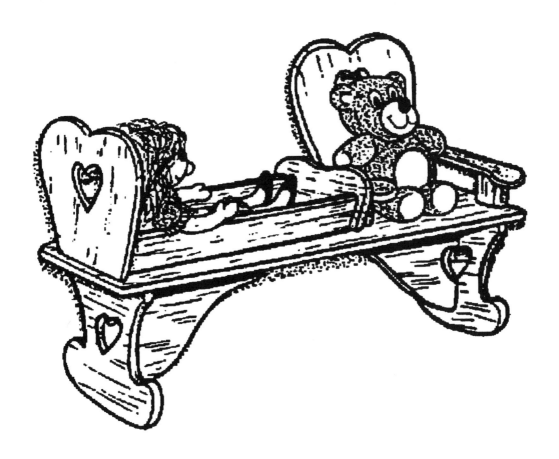

This is the finished project. It's certain to please the young recipient. Also, teddy bears like to rock too.

NOTES AND CALCULATIONS

Sweetheart Door Harp

This project welcomes all callers with a cascade of music as the little balls bounce off the strings stretched over the music chamber. This is a relatively easy weekend project and requires a minimum of tools to complete. You better make a couple because you're certain to get a bunch of requests for more.

MATERIALS

⅛" plywood 2 board feet
    1 piece 9" x 11" heart back
    1 piece 9" x 11" heart facing

1x12 white pine
    1 piece 9" x 11" heart body

HARDWARE AND MISCELLANEOUS

Small picture hanger
10 tuning pins
5 clapper balls
5 feet music wire .016 thickness
50" thin monofilament
Carpenter's or Titebond glue
5 pieces wood dowel ¼" x 2"
Small bottles of acrylic enamel,
  colors of your choice
5 round toothpicks

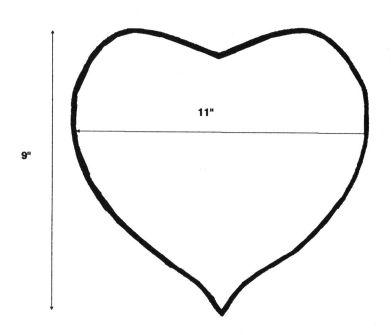

THE BACK IS CUT FROM THIN PLYWOOD

TOOLS REQUIRED

Drill with ¼" and ⅛" bits
Saber or coping saw
Clamps
Sander, pad or belt
Pliers

INSTRUCTIONS

1. Enlarge the heart-shaped patterns to the size specified above. You can easily make your own patterns by folding a piece of cardboard in half and drawing half the heart shape on the fold and then cutting to size with scissors.

2. Trace the heart facing and backing designs onto the ⅛" plywood and cut to size. Do the same with the heart body design on the 1" lumber. Cut the center heart pieces.

3. You are about to make a sandwich of the wood pieces by placing the plywood pieces on the

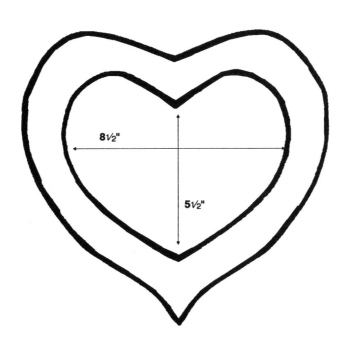

THE CENTER HEART IS CUT FROM 1" LUMBER

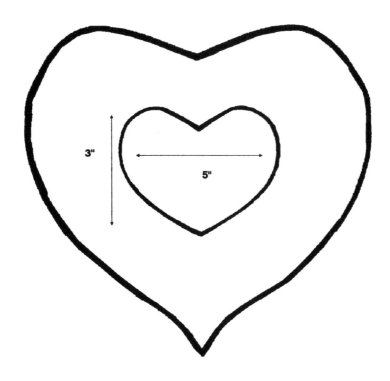

3"

5"

THE HEART FACING IS CUT FROM THIN PLYWOOD

front and back of the body piece. Glue them in place and clamp securely.

4. Sand the edges of the assembly, rounding it slightly.

5. Drill ¼" holes for the wood dowels at the top of the assembly and at the sides for the tuning pins. Double check the thickness of the tuning pins as you may

need a different diameter drill bit.

6. Paint the project the color of your choice.

7. Drill tiny holes in the center of the wood dowels and the clapper balls, using a small wire brad as a drill bit. If you have a pointed drill bit such as the kind on countersink bits, it will serve the same purpose.

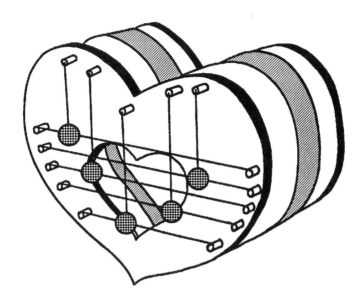

THE HARP IS ACTUALLY A HOLLOW WOOD SANDWICH

8. Attach lengths of monofilament into the holes with glue. Tap the pointed end of a round toothpick into the hole and break it off flush with the tip of the wood dowel.

9. Insert the tuning pins in the sides and attach the music wire. Turn the pins with pliers to fit them into the holes and to tighten the wire to the pitch you prefer.

10. Cut the monofilament to size and attach the clapper balls using glue and round toothpicks to hold the monofilament in place in the wood balls.

11. Attach a small picture hanger in the back of the project and hang it on the wall or door of your choice.

You can make many variations of the basic project in many sizes, shapes and designs.

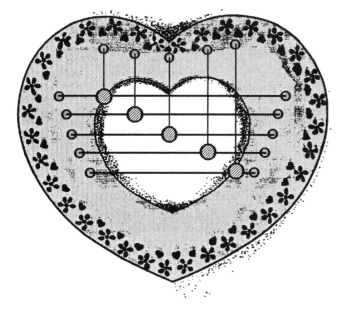

Here are two examples of design variations. Feel free to add any number of wood designs to the basic concept. Just remember it's a hollow wood sandwich. Now it's time to go find your sweetheart and say, SURPRISE!

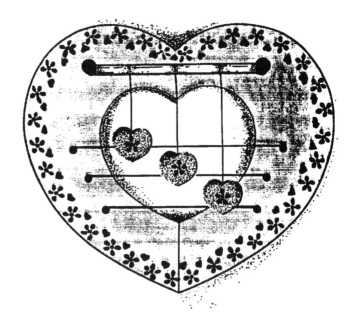

Kitchen and Patio Chopping Block/Serving Cart

This rolling work center contains a large surface area for chopping foods and a cutting board for smaller projects. It also includes a hidden salad bowl and a storage area for potatoes or onions or charcoal. It takes little space and yet it is one of the most functional projects that you will ever put on your patio or in your kitchen.

MATERIALS

2x4 white pine 75 linear feet
    15 pieces 36" long chopping
      surface
    5 pieces 31" long, shelf
    4 pieces 26½ " leg
    4 pieces 1½ "x 2" x 26½" leg pieces
    8 pieces 1½" x 2¾" x 2¾" leg ends
    1 piece 1½ " x 1½" x 5" bin handle
    1 piece 1⅛ " x 1½" x 1¼" bin pivot

2x8 white pine 18" length
    2 pieces 7" diameter wheels

1x8 white pine 6 linear feet
    2 pieces 3" x 13⅜ counter brace
    2 pieces 3" x 17½ shelf supports
    1 piece ¾" x ¾" x 6½" bin pivot
    1 piece 5" x 11" bin floor
    4 pieces ¾" x ¾" x 1½" filler block
    1 piece ¾" x ¾" x 9¼" bin stop

½" plywood 2' x 4'
    2 pieces bin sides (see pattern)
    1 piece 11" x 11" bin back
    1 piece 13" x 14⅝ bin front

¾" hardwood oak and walnut
    2 board feet
    18 pieces ¾" x ¾" x 20" cutting
    board (see pattern)

HARDWARE AND MISCELLANEOUS

2 carriage bolts ½" x 4"
    2 swivel casters (optional)
    Medium size bottle Carpenter's or
      Titebond glue
    16 screws 2½"
    60 screws 1½ "
    20 finishing nails ¾"
    ½" wood dowel bin pivot 4"
    2 shaker pegs 2"
    13" diameter salad bowl
      stainless steel
    12 wood plugs ½"
    2 finishing nails 1½ "
    1 wood dowel 1" x 24" handle

TOOLS REQUIRED

Circular saw
    Saber saw with long blade
    Pipe clamps
    Drill with countersink bit
      ½" and ¼" drill bits
    Screwdriver
    Router with rounding over,
      cove and rabbeting bits
    Hammer and nail set

INSTRUCTIONS

1. Measure and cut the 2x4 boards forming the chopping block top. This is made of fifteen 2x4s cut to 36" length.

2. Glue and clamp the boards as shown.

3. Lay out the recess for the salad bowl and cutting board. Use the outline for the cutting board as a pattern (13" diameter). Lay the salad bowl in the center of this outline and draw a circle the diameter of the outside lip of the salad bowl. Next measure the underside of the lip and redraw the center circle to accommodate that lip. The idea is for the salad bowl to fit on the edge of the rabbet joint you are about to cut. You can use any size salad bowl you wish. Simply modify the size for the cutting board so that it is almost 1" wider than the diameter of the salad bowl minus the lip.

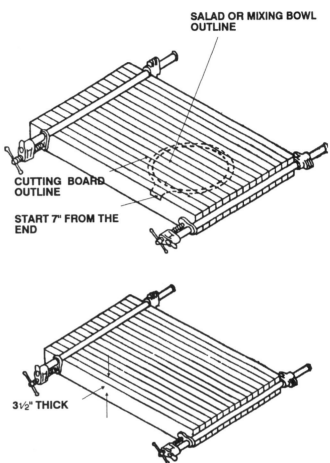

4. Drill a ½" starter hole and cut out the center circle using a saber saw.

5. Using a router with a rabbeting bit, rout a ½" rabbet, ¾" deep

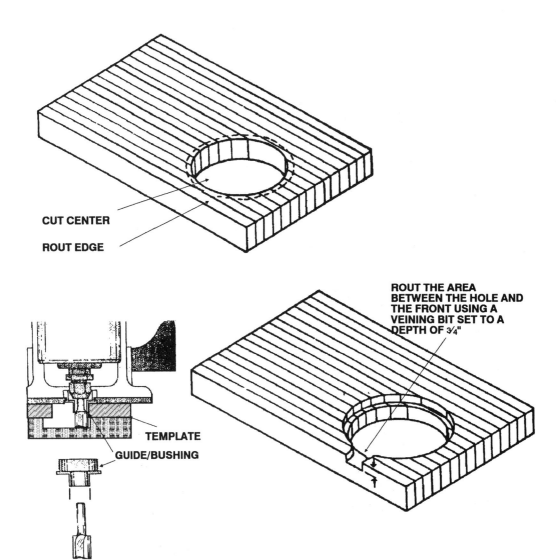

CUT CENTER

ROUT EDGE

ROUT THE AREA BETWEEN THE HOLE AND THE FRONT USING A VEINING BIT SET TO A DEPTH OF ¾"

TEMPLATE

GUIDE/BUSHING

around the center circle. Drop the salad bowl into this cutout, the lip should fit over the edge, holding the bowl in place.

6. Using a router with a ½ " veining bit, rout the recess for the cutting board handle to a depth of ¾". I

suggest you make a jig or template for this operation because to try it freehand is almost certain to invite a mistake. Use a guide bushing in the router that will follow the template outline.

7. Measure and cut the two counter support boards from 1x8 pine. Center 1" from each end of the underside of the counter and attach 1½" screws into each of the 2x4 boards.

8. Measure and cut the shelf assembly. This consists of five 2x4s cut to a length of 31" and butt joined. Glue and clamp the assembly. Measure and cut the two support boards from 1x8 stock and glue and screw to the underside of the shelf. Make certain you put two screws into each 2x4 through the 1" stock. Set aside to dry.

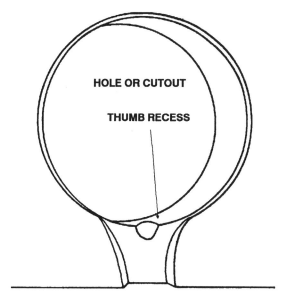

HOLE OR CUTOUT

THUMB RECESS

CROSS SECTION OF THE COUNTER TOP

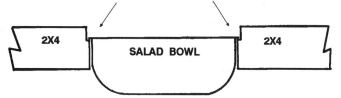

CUTTING BOARD FITS HERE

2X4

SALAD BOWL

2X4

ATTACH SUPPORTS TO THE UNDERSIDE OF THE COUNTERTOP TO AVOID SEPARATION OF THE 2X4 BOARDS. ATTACH 1" FROM EACH END

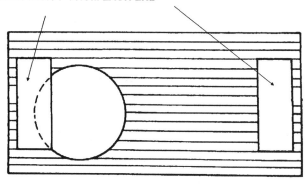

9. Measure and cut the boards forming the leg assemblies. The assembly consists of two 2x4's cut to a length of 26½". One 2x4 is cut to a width of 2". Cut rabbets into both ends of each leg part ¾" x 1½". Assemble the leg using glue and screws forming an L-shape. Measure and cut the leg blocks and

SHELF ASSEMBLY

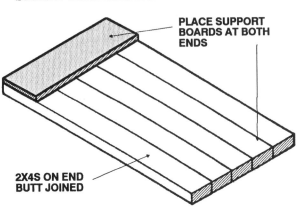

PLACE SUPPORT BOARDS AT BOTH ENDS

2X4S ON END BUTT JOINED

LEG ASSEMBLY

LEG

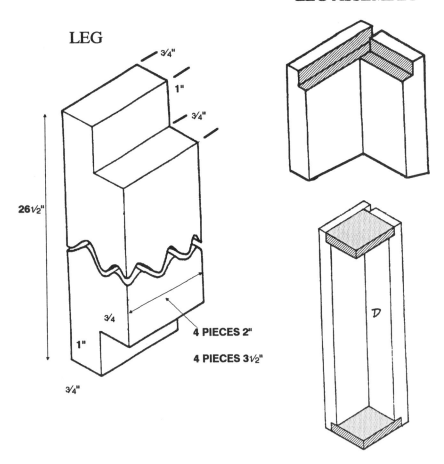

26½"

¾"

1"

¾"

¾

1"

¾"

4 PIECES 2"

4 PIECES 3½"

D

glue and screw into the ends of the leg assembly.

10. Attach the legs to the support blocks on the bottom of the counter using glue and screws. Attach the shelf to the legs 14½" below the counter bottom using screws and glue.

11. Measure and cut the bin pieces from the ½" plywood. Cut the bottom from 1x8 pine stock. Assemble the structure using ¾" finishing nails and glue. Countersink the nails and fill the holes with wood filler, sanding smooth.

12. The bin fits to the left of the shelf, mounted on a pivot made up of a ½" wood dowel and two bin pivots made by drilling a ½" hole into wood stock as shown and then cutting the block in half. Glue the pivot blocks and wood dowel pieces into position as

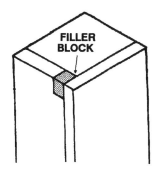

FILLER BLOCK

INSTALL THE LEGS NEXT TO THE SUPPORT BLOCKS 1" FROM EACH END

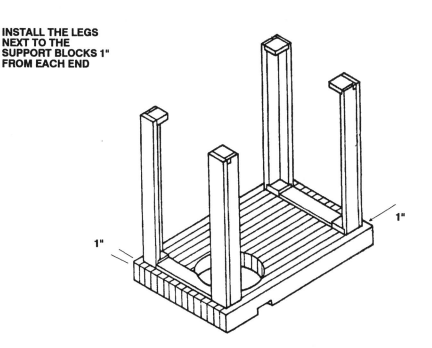

1"

1"

AT THIS POINT, IT IS YOUR BASIC CHOPPING BLOCK

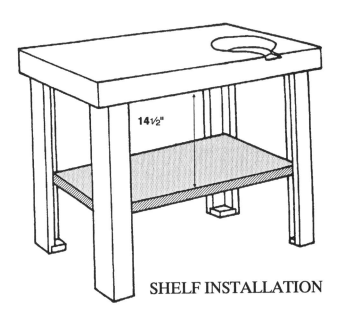

14½"

SHELF INSTALLATION

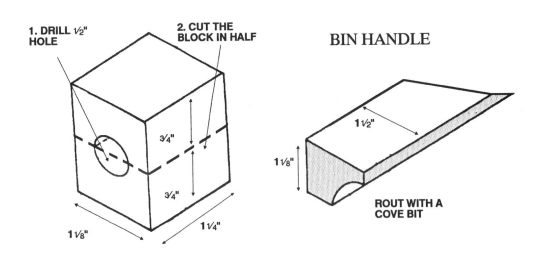

1. DRILL ½" HOLE

2. CUT THE BLOCK IN HALF

¾"

¾"

1⅛"

1¼"

BIN HANDLE

1½"

1⅛"

ROUT WITH A COVE BIT

BIN ASSEMBLY

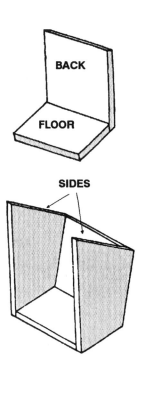

BACK

FLOOR

SIDES

1 SQUARE = 1 INCH

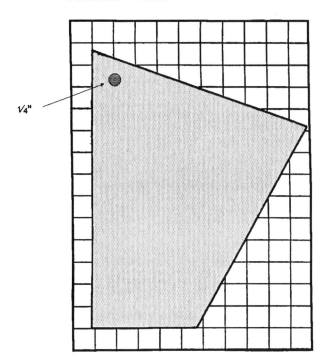

1/4"

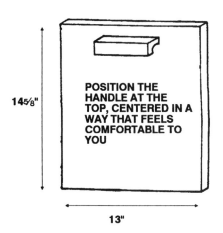

14 5/8"

13"

POSITION THE
HANDLE AT THE
TOP, CENTERED IN A
WAY THAT FEELS
COMFORTABLE TO
YOU

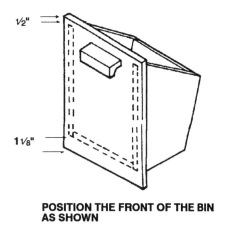

1/2"

1 1/8"

POSITION THE FRONT OF THE BIN
AS SHOWN

BIN STOP INSTALLATION

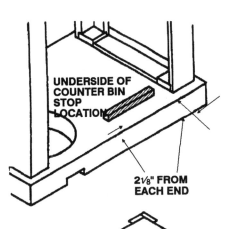

UNDERSIDE OF COUNTER BIN STOP LOCATION

2⅛" FROM EACH END

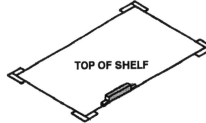

TOP OF SHELF

POSITION DOWEL PIVOTS SO BIN FITS CLOSE AGAINST LEFT LEG OR WHEREVER YOU WANT IT TO PIVOT

BIN PIVOT BLOCK INSTALLATION

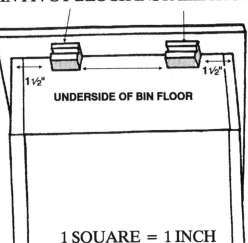

1½"   1½"

UNDERSIDE OF BIN FLOOR

1 SQUARE = 1 INCH

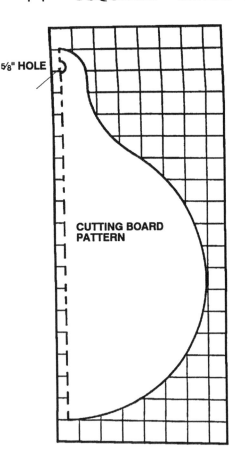

⅝" HOLE

CUTTING BOARD PATTERN

shown on the shelf and bottom of the bin.

13. Measure and cut the bin stop board and attach to the underside of the counter as shown. Measure and cut the bin handle and rout the edge using a cove bit to form a lip. Attach it to the front of the bin using screws and glue.

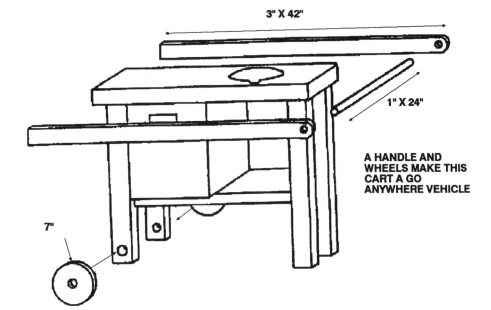

3" X 42"

1" X 24"

**A HANDLE AND
WHEELS MAKE THIS
CART A GO
ANYWHERE VEHICLE**

7"

**THERE ARE MANY POSSIBLE VARIATIONS
ON THE BASIC CART IDEA. PICK ONE THAT
FITS YOUR LIFE STYLE**

14. This design was intended to have 2 ½" high casters at one end and wheels on the other. If you opt to omit the casters, shorten the legs containing the wheels to the appropriate length or lengthen the legs containing the casters, depending on the height you prefer. If you plan to use the casters, attach them to the rear legs now.

15. Measure and cut the two wood wheels from 2x8 wood stock, 7" diameter. Drill a ½" hole in the center. Position the wheels on the front legs, drill a ½" hole into the leg and attach the wheels using carriage bolts. Make certain the counter top is level when you do this step.

16. Measure and cut the wood handle sides from 1x4 wood stock. These are cut 3" wide and 42" long. Drill a 1" hole at the end of side of the handles as shown. Measure and cut the handle from 1" wood dowel stock. Attach the handle and the sides using screws and glue. Note: countersink the screw holes and fill with wood plugs after the screws are tightened. Nail 1½" finishing nails into the ends of the handle sides to hold the wood dowel in place. Cut a notch for the cutting board

handle and rout the edge of the cutting board inset with a rounding over bit.

17. The cutting board is made from laminations of hardwood. You may opt to make it from solid wood, which will warp after time, or from ¾" plywood instead. I laminated alternating strips of ¾" oak and walnut and then cut the assembly to shape. I then routed the edges using a rounding over bit.

18. Go over the entire project, filling recesses with wood filler and sanding smooth.

19. You can stain the project, the color of your choice. If you plan to use the top surface for cutting food, use regular vegetable oil instead of stain to cover the surface.

NOTES AND CALCULATIONS

Sweetheart Settle

Don't wait to make your love connection—start your own with this project. This is a unique settle that will stand out anywhere you put it. In a foyer, hallway or entrance to your home, it will say, this house has class. You can make two different adaptations of this project. I chose to make one that has a storage bench under the seat. If you don't like having heavy furniture in the house that can't be moved often, you may opt to not add the storage area. In any event, people will ooh and aah when they see this Sweetheart Settle.

MATERIALS

This project is made from ¾" red oak lumber and veneer coated plywood. It can be made from any wood you choose; however, the richness of red oak seems to make this project stand out from most of the other woods. If you want to give it an Early American look, use pine instead. The sides, front and seating area are made from splined pieces. Refer to the tips and techniques section if you need help in this area.

¾" red oak 40 square feet
    2 pieces 18" x 60" sides
    1 piece 16" x 48" front
    1 piece 15" x 48" seat
    1 piece 10" x 53½" top
    2 pieces 3" x 48" bottom
      trim
    2 pieces 3" x 43" side trim
    1 piece 3" 48" seat back

¾" red oak veneer core
    plywood 48" x 80"
    1 piece 48" x 60" back
    1 piece 15" x 48" floor

1x3 pine 22 linear feet
    2 pieces 2" x 48" front seat
      support boards
    2 pieces 2" x 13½" side seat
      supports
    2 pieces 1" x 48" front floor
      supports
    2 pieces 1" x 13½" side floor
      supports

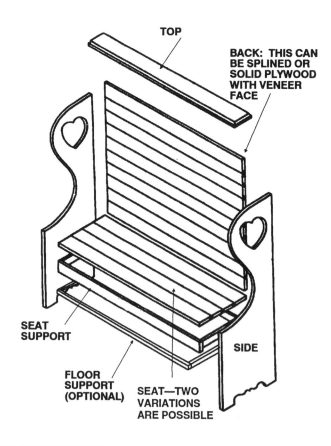

TOP

BACK: THIS CAN BE SPLINED OR SOLID PLYWOOD WITH VENEER FACE

SEAT SUPPORT

FLOOR SUPPORT (OPTIONAL)

SEAT—TWO VARIATIONS ARE POSSIBLE

SIDE

HARDWARE AND MISCELLANEOUS

100 screws 1½" drywall type
100 wood plugs oak ½"
Carpenter's or Titebond glue
2 hinges brass 3"
1 quart Danish oil stain, dark
  walnut

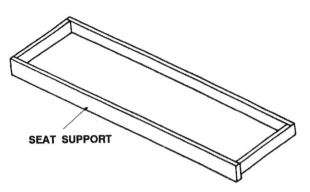

SEAT SUPPORT

TOOLS REQUIRED

Saber saw
Circular saw
Drill with ½" bit and
  countersink
Router with rounding over
  and cove bits
Belt or pad sander

INSTRUCTIONS

1. There are two variations of the basic settle, one with a storage area and one with a plain seat. Decide which you are going to make before proceeding. Measure and cut the wood pieces forming the sides from the ¾" red oak solid wood and the back and floor from the veneer core red oak plywood. Using a router with a rounding over bit, rout the front edge of the sides and both sides of the heart cutout.

ONE SQUARE = 1 INCH

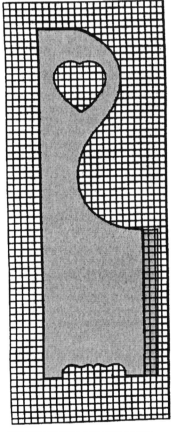

**THE SIDE CAN BE 16" OR 18"
WIDE AT THE BASE . USE 18" FOR
THE STORAGE VERSION**

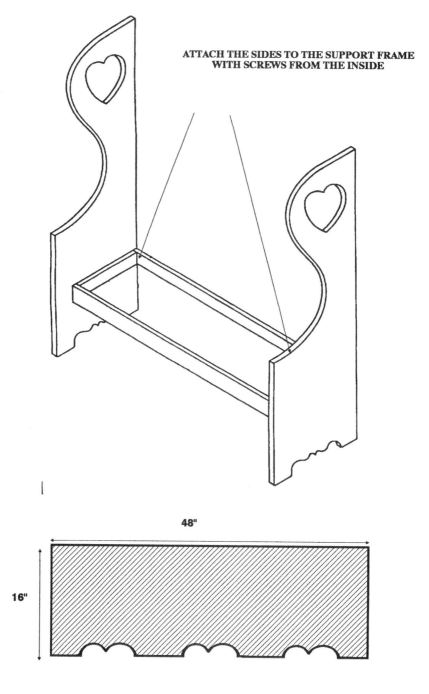

**ATTACH THE SIDES TO THE SUPPORT FRAME
WITH SCREWS FROM THE INSIDE**

48"

16"

COPY THIS DESIGN FOR THE LOWER FRONT

2. Measure and cut the pieces forming the seat and floor supports from the 1x3 pine lumber.

3. Assemble the seat and floor support frames using screws and glue.

4. Attach the back, floor support and seat support to the sides using glue and screws. Use screws through the inside of the floor and seat supports into the sides. Use a countersink to pre-drill screw holes through the sides into the back. Insert the screws, cap the holes with wood plugs and sand flush.

5. If you only plan to make the seat version of this project, cut the seat to full size of 18" x 48", not the size specified in the materials list. Rout the front edge with a rounding over bit and router. Lay it on top of the seat support and butt it against the back. Attach using screws and glue. Cut a facing board from oak, 1" wider than the front of the seat support board and

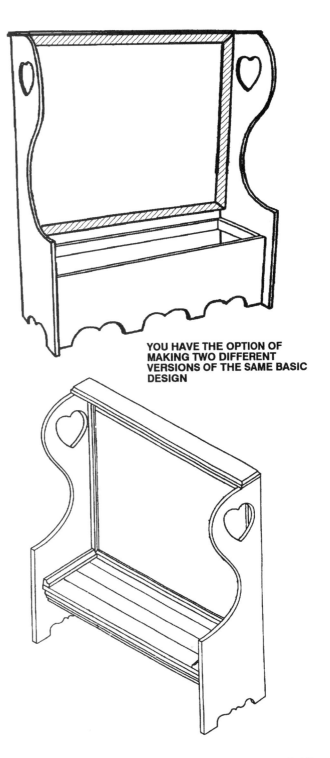

YOU HAVE THE OPTION OF MAKING TWO DIFFERENT VERSIONS OF THE SAME BASIC DESIGN

screw and glue in place on the seat facing board directly underneath the seat. Add the molding and the top and you're done. If you want to make the storage version, read on.

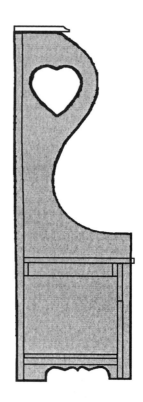

6. Measure and cut the top and the front of the settle from red oak. Rout the top on the sides and front with a router and a cove bit. Rout the bottom curved sections with a router and a rounding over bit.

7. Attach the top so that it is centered on the sides at the top and flush against the back. Use screws, glue and wood plugs, etc.

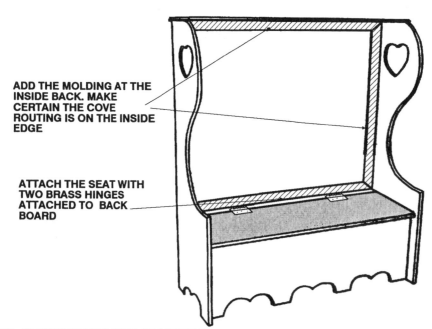

ADD THE MOLDING AT THE INSIDE BACK. MAKE CERTAIN THE COVE ROUTING IS ON THE INSIDE EDGE

ATTACH THE SEAT WITH TWO BRASS HINGES ATTACHED TO BACK BOARD

8. Attach the front using screws, glue and wood plugs; sand flush.

9. Measure and cut the seat and the seat back board.

10. Attach the seat backboard on top of the seat support and butted against the back. Attach with screws and glue, fill the holes with wood plugs and sand flush. Attach the seat to the back board using brass hinges. Note: You may wish to shorten the length of the seat to avoid contact with the sides when you raise it.

11. Measure and cut the molding pieces. Rout on the inside edge with a cove bit and a router. Miter the corners and attach to the inside of the back.

12. Stain the project the color of your choice. Go find a sweetheart and check it out.

NOTES AND CALCULATIONS

Rolltop Bread Box

This is one of those weekend workshop projects you will hand down to your kids, and, of course, they will consider it an antique. Actually it will be by the time they get it. I made this project from walnut, although any wood will do. It is a dress rehearsal for making a really big project like a rolltop desk. This will keep the bread from drying out and will brighten your kitchen as well.

MATERIALS

¾" walnut 9 square feet
  2 pieces 13½ " x 14" sides
  1 piece 4" x 15⅜" top
  1 piece 13 3/4" x 13¾" back
  2 pieces 9½ " x 14¼" shelves
  2 pieces 3" x 9" shelf stops
  1 piece 2" x 13½" front
  1 piece ⅝" x 13½" handle
  27 pieces ⅜ " x ¾" x 14¼"
    tambour slat

HARDWARE AND MISCELLANEOUS

  1 piece scrap wood/plywood
    14" x 16" router jig
  1 piece burlap or canvas
    14½" x 19½" tambour form
  24 wood screws 1¼"
  4 screws ½" flathead
  Carpenter's or Titebond glue
  Danish oil clear

TOOLS REQUIRED

  Circular saw
  Screwdriver
  Drill with countersink and
    ¼" bits
  Wood plug cutter ½"
  Router with guide bushing,
    rounding over bit, veining
    bit and ⅛" slot cutter

Saber saw
Chisel ½ "
Pipe or bar clamps 18" long

INSTRUCTIONS

NOTE: I suggest you enlarge the drawings shown to the necessary size using an enlarging copy machine. Also, the sides for the bread box need to be made from splined wood pieces, ensuring that the splined do not intersect the areas that will house the tambour.

1. Measure and cut to size all of the wood pieces as listed.

2. The tambour door slides into the two side pieces. To accommodate the door you must cut a groove ¼" deep and ½" wide into each side piece as shown in the dotted line area on the pattern. Additional grooves need to be cut to house the shelves as well. Because the grooves must be cut in a fairly exact manner, it is advisable to make a jig for this purpose. To make the jig, take a piece of ¼" plywood and transfer the pattern design and placement of the tambour and shelf grooves. Cut out the plywood areas transferred to the plywood using a

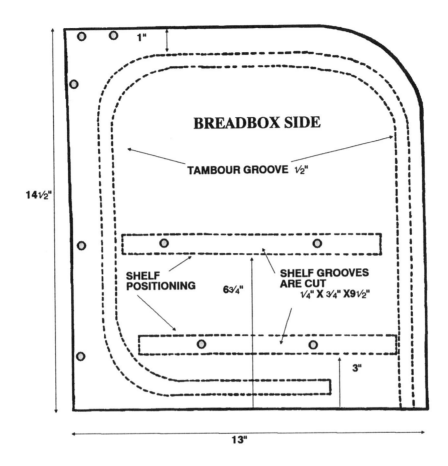

BREADBOX SIDE

TAMBOUR GROOVE ½"

14½"

SHELF POSITIONING

SHELF GROOVES ARE CUT ¼" X ¾" X9½"

6¾"

3"

13"

saber saw. Tack the plywood pattern to one side, positioning it properly so the slots are in the proper place on the wood sides. Rout the slots using a router with a guide bushing and a veining bit. To use the jig for the opposite side, turn it over and tack it to the other side piece making it a mirror image of the first. (The two sides need to be mirror images). The shapely curved section of

each groove should be cut slightly wider than the straight groove section to accommodate the tambours as they round the bend. The grooves cut for the shelves must be exactly ¾" x 9" wide and ¼" deep. Use a chisel to square the corners of the shelf groove.

3. Measure and cut dados in both ends of the top piece, $\frac{3}{8}$" wide and $\frac{5}{8}$" deep as shown.

4. Attach the shelf stop boards on the two shelves, centered $\frac{1}{4}$" from each end as shown. Attach using screws and glue.

5. Assemble the sides, back, shelves, and top as shown. Glue and clamp the pieces securely. Drill counter-sink holes through the sides into the top, back, and shelves and insert the screws.

6. Using a drill with a $\frac{1}{2}$" plug cutter, cut 18 plugs from scrap wood. Glue the wood plugs into the counter-sink holes and sand flush.

7. The sliding door consists of narrow slats (tambours) glued in parallel to a piece of canvas or burlap. The slats are $\frac{3}{8}$" x $\frac{3}{4}$" x 14, with one side slightly rounded. The easiest way to make these slats is to cut a board to length (14 $\frac{1}{4}$"). Next rout the length of

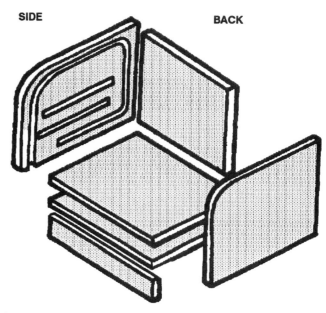

SIDE   BACK

LOOKS COMPLICATED BUT IT'S NOT. THE COMPONENTS FIT TOGETHER EASILY.

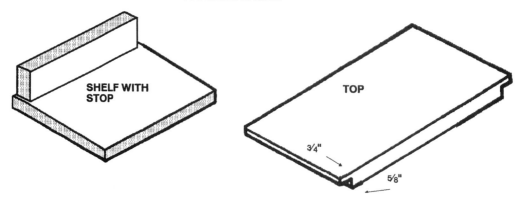

SHELF WITH STOP

TOP

$\frac{3}{4}$"

$\frac{5}{8}$"

the face of the board on both sides with a rounding over bit. Next, cut the slat to width (⅜"). Continue doing this until you have 27 pieces.

8. Position the pieces as shown on top of a piece of burlap or canvas that is centered about 1 inch short on each end and at least 1 inch wider on both ends of the width of the tambours when laid side by side. Clamp the tambours using two pieces of wood scraps as shown, clamped on the ends. The tambours should be snug or as tight side by side as you can make them. Apply some wax paper on top of the fabric and add a board that covers the fabric. Add a heavy weight or a series of clamps to hold the assembly tight. It is extremely important that the weight be even and that the fabric is glued securely to the wood slats. Be careful to not let any glue into the sides of the slats or you

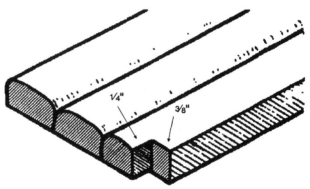

TAMBOURS SHOULD BE CLAMPED TIGHT AND CLOSE TOGETHER

CANVAS

WOOD SCRAPS

SLATS

will have a rolltop door with terminal rigor mortis.

9. To make a door stop, cut a notch from each end of the first tambour slat that is ¼" x ⅜". Use these

pieces as door stops to keep the tambour from falling out once in place.

10. Cut the door handle to shape as shown. Center it on the second tambour and attach using glue and screws from the back.

11. Insert the sliding door into the slot at the bottom of the bread box assembly. Make certain it rolls up and down smoothly. Adding some beeswax to the grooves will aid this process. Attach the door stops into the bottom of the front groove using glue and screws.

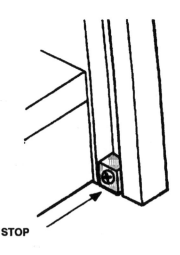

ROLLTOP DOOR
HANDLE

¼"

13½"

**PLACE HANDLE
ON SECOND
TAMBOUR FROM
THE BOTTOM**

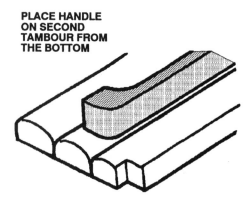

STOP

12. I finished the project using a clear Danish oil. This brings out the texture and grain of the walnut, plus it acts as a sealer.

13. Roll up the door, insert the bread and you're done.

NOTES AND CALCULATIONS

Bunny Bandit and Calico Gal
Wall Hanging

This is one of those projects that I was forced to design. Not your average woodworking project, nonetheless, for those of you into bunnies, it is certainly different. This is a nice wall hanging that works well in a hall or foyer. It says, Welcome, this is a nice place to visit.

MATERIALS

1x6 ash 6 linear feet
    1 piece 4" x 27" back
    1 piece 3" x 23" shelf
    1 piece 4" x 4" bracket
    2 pieces 5" x 8" bunnies
    1 piece 4" x 4" heart

HARDWARE AND MISCELLANEOUS

10 eye hooks small
4 screws 1½" drywall variety
2 wood plugs ½"
Carpenter's or Titebond glue
1 pint blue translucent
   acrylic stain
Monofilament or string,
   approximately 48"

TOOLS REQUIRED

Saber saw
Circular saw
Drill with ⅛" and coun-
tersink bits
Router with cove bit
Screwdriver

INSTRUCTIONS

1. Using a copying machine with enlarging capability, enlarge the
patterns for the rabbits, heart and
bracket. You do not need to be
perfect with this, just get roughly
to the sizes specified.

2. Trace your patterns onto the
wood pieces and cut to size using
a sabre saw.

3. Using a circular saw, cut the shelf
and back boards. Cut a 1½" quarter moon or circle notch in the

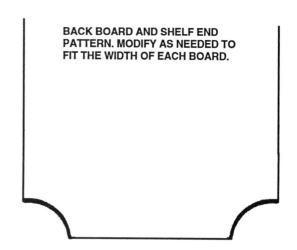

BACK BOARD AND SHELF END PATTERN. MODIFY AS NEEDED TO FIT THE WIDTH OF EACH BOARD.

ends of the back and one end of the shelf using a saber saw.

4. Rout all sides of the back board and the sides and the front of the shelf using a cove bit.

5. Attach the shelf board, along with the bracket centered, to the back board approximately 8" from the top. Use screws and glue.

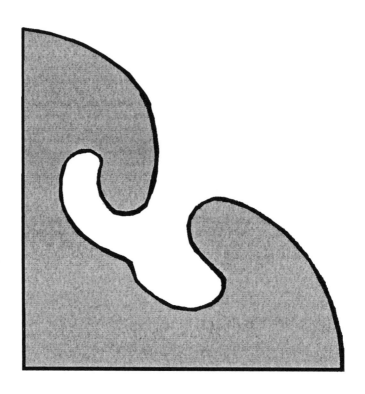

FULL SIZE PATTERN

6. Sand the heart and rabbit pieces to slightly round the edges.

7. Stain all of the wood pieces and allow them to dry thoroughly.

8. Attach the rabbits and the heart to the back and shelf assembly using monofilament or string.

9. Drill a countersunk screw hole on the front of the back board 2" from each end and mount on the wall of your choice. Fill the screw holes with wood plugs. Do not glue, but do stain.

10. Stand back and wait for the applause. Don't wait forever, though.

ENLARGE PATTERN TO FULL SIZE AND TRACE ON WOOD

SUSPEND
RABBITS AND
HEART WITH
THIN
MONOFILAMENT

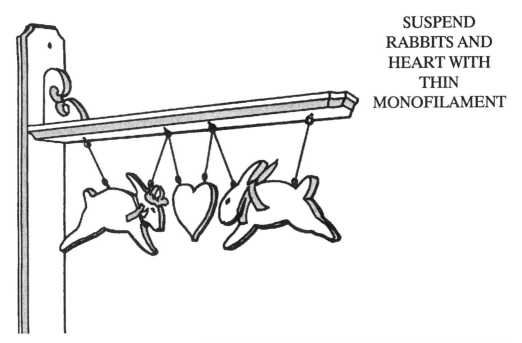

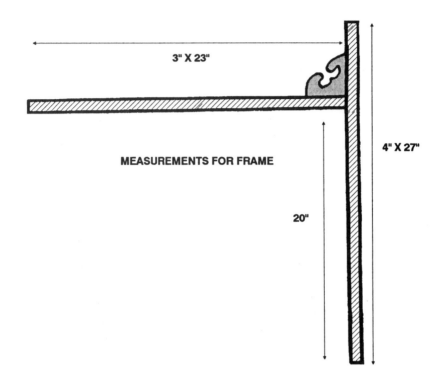

3" X 23"

MEASUREMENTS FOR FRAME

4" X 27"

20"

Game Table/Cabinet

This is a project that adds a special touch to any room in which it sits. The top serves as a playing surface for chess or checkers, and the cabinet serves as storage for other games and entertainment items. You can store video cassettes and electronic game cartridges as well. This is a weekend project that is sure to please everyone in the family.

MATERIALS

1x18 splined white pine 14 linear feet
- 2 pieces 15⅝" x 23½" sides
- 1 piece 15" x 23½" back
- 1 piece 12 ⅝" square table top center
- 2 pieces 3⅜" x 17" table top sides
- 2 pieces 2¼" x 12⅝" table top front and back
- 2 pieces 1¾" x 16¼" side molding
- 1 piece 1¾" x 17⅝" front molding
- 1 piece 14¼" x 15" bottom shelf
- 2 pieces 2¼" x 23½" front side facing
- 1 piece 3" x 12⅛" bottom facing
- 1 piece 3½" x 12⅛" top facing
- 2 pieces 1" x 15" shelf supports
- 2 pieces 12" x 1⅝" top and bottom door frame
- 2 pieces 17" x 1⅝" door frame sides

2x4 white pine 18 linear inches
- 6 pieces ¼" x 1½" x 18" door strips
- 4 pieces ¼" x ½" x 10" door strip backing

HARDWARE AND MISCELLANEOUS

Carpenter's or Titebond glue
40 wood screws 1½" drywall type
40 wood plugs ½"
2 hinges 2" brass with screws
1 pint paint or stain of your choice
20 biscuit splines any size will do
8 wire brads ¾"

TOOLS REQUIRED

Drill with countersink bit
Screwdriver
Pad or belt sander
Band saw (optional)
Circular saw or table saw
Biscuit joiner
Pipe or bar clamps and web clamp

INSTRUCTIONS

If you are unable to obtain 1x18" spline pine you will have to create your own for the sides, shelf, top and back from 1x12 stock.

1. Measure and cut the sides, back, shelf and shelf support pieces.

2. Assemble the back and sides as shown. Predrill screw holes with a countersink. Attach the sides to the back using screws and glue.

3. Measure and cut the facing pieces and assemble the front of the project by splining the sides to the top and bottom pieces. Glue and clamp.

4. Attach the shelf supports at the bottom so that the shelf is level with the top of the bottom facing piece. Attach the self supports using glue and screws. Attach the shelf to the top of this assembly.

5. Attach the facing assembly to the front of the project using screws and glue. Glue wood plugs into all of the screw holes and sand smooth.

6. Using a router with a rounding over bit, rout the door opening,

THE SIDES ARE 15⅝" WIDE, THE BACK IS 15" WIDE AND BOTH ARE 23½" HIGH

bottom and side edges of the project.

7. Measure and cut the molding pieces to size. Rout the bottom edge of the molding pieces with a router and a cove bit. Note: you may want to rout the piece first and then cut to size.

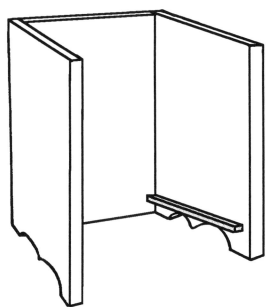

ATTACH THE SIDES TO THE BACK

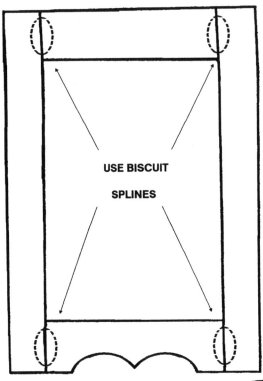

USE BISCUIT

SPLINES

9. Measure and cut the pieces forming the top. The checker squares in the center top piece are created with a table saw blade set to a ⅛" depth of cut. Most saw blades are about ⅛" thick, so you will have a square of 1½". Set the saw so that you first cut the center of the board. Make one pass and then a second creating a + in the board with four squares. Cut into the center of each of these squares and repeat the process creating four more +'s. Set the saw to cut across the center of these squares and again create the + figure. By doing this you

8. Attach the molding to the top sides and front of the project using screws and glue.

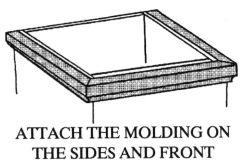

ATTACH THE MOLDING ON THE SIDES AND FRONT

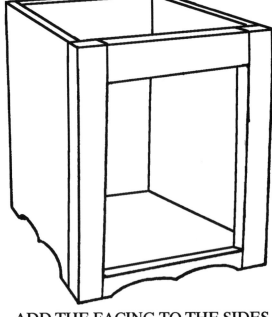

ADD THE FACING TO THE SIDES

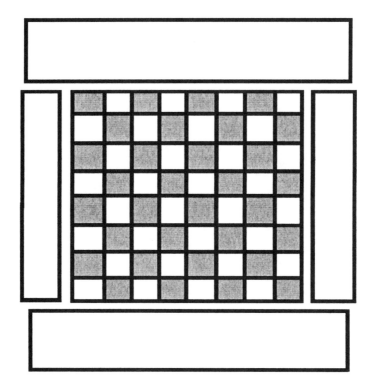

CHESS SET CONSISTS OF 5 PIECES OF 1" LUMBER

SAW KERFS FORM THE CHECKER SQUARES

will have cut all of the squares necessary to make up the playing area. Next set the saw so that you make a ⅛" cut on the very edge of the board and obtain a ⅛" x ⅛" dado. You should now have 64, hopefully even, squares on the

top of the board. Sand this board to remove all splinters.

10. Glue the top center, side, front and back pieces forming a flat uniform block. You can try butt gluing the pieces, however, I

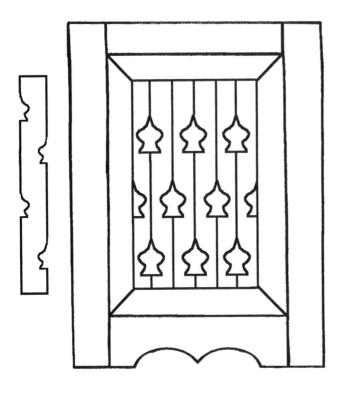

FRONT AND DOOR ASSEMBLY

recommend using biscuit splines
or blind splines that you cut yourself.

11. While the top is gluing up, cut the
    wood strips that form the door as-
    sembly. Do this first by cutting a
    strip of wood 1⅝" wide. Next rout
    one edge of the board with a rou-
    ter and a rabbeting bit set to cre-
    ate a dado ½" wide and ¼" deep.
    Next cut the miters that form the
    separate pieces. Make certain
    that the dado is on the inside cut

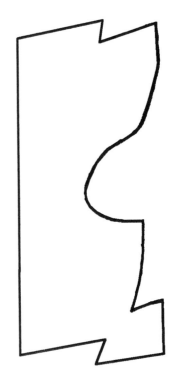

SPADE PATTERN IS FULL
SIZE

as this is where the center pieces will fit in the final assembly.

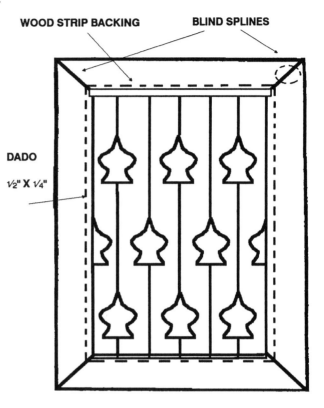

WOOD STRIP BACKING   **BLIND SPLINES**

DADO

½" X ¼"

12. Cut small blind splines in the edges of the door pieces and glue and clamp them together forming the door assembly. I suggest the use of a web clamp for this purpose.

13. Center and attach the top so that the back of the top is flush with the back of the cabinet. Fill the screw holes with wood plugs and sand smooth. There should be roughly a ¾" lip around the sides and front.

14. Rout the edges of the top using a router with a rounding over bit.

15. Rout the outside edge of the door with a router and a rounding over bit.

16. Measure and cut the pieces that form the spade designs in the door inset. This is done by drawing half of the spade on the edge of a 2x4 cut to size. Using a band saw or coping saw, cut out the pieces. Next rip ¼" strips from the 2x4, forming the strips necess-ary to make the pattern in the door. Sand these pieces to remove all rough edges.

17. Place the strips into the door inset, flipping every other one to form the spade figure. Glue them in place and place wood strips at the top and bottom and in the center to hold them in place. Attach with ¾" wire brads nailed into the door frame.

18. Attach the door to the cabinet using 2" brass hinges or any decorative hinge that you prefer. Next attach a door knob in the center left of the door frame and a magnetic catch at the bottom. The door should stop against the bottom shelf.

19. Stain or paint the project the color of your choice.

Mirrored
Candle Sconce

Blanket Chest

Game Table Cabinet

Forever Calendar Clock

Tavern
Lantern

Sweetheart Settle

Magazine Rack Tissue Dispenser

Sweetheart Mirror

Childs Rocker/Doll Cradle

Sconce

Teddy Bear Settle Toy Chest

Birdhouse Cookie Jar

Corner Shelves

Curved Back Chairs and Rocker

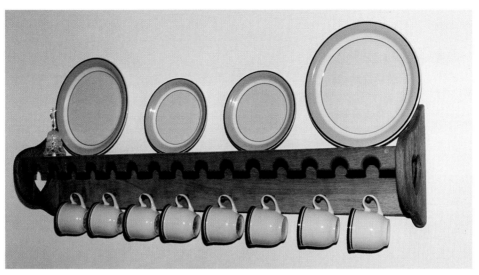

Plate and Cup Rack

Bunny Bandit and Calico Gal Wall Hanging

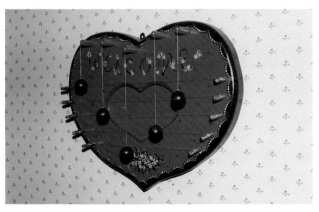

Sweetheart Door Harp

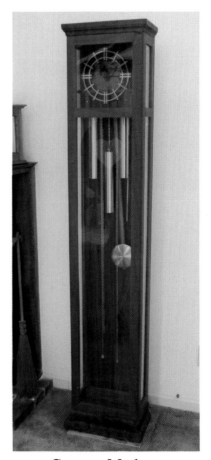

Country Modern
Grandfather Clock

Rolltop Bread Box

Checkerboard Game and
Coffee Table

Chopping Block Serving Cart

Deacon's Bench

Hanging Sweetheart
Lamp

Sweetheart Magazine Rack

**Paper Cup
Dispenser**

Sweetheart Shadow Box

Tulip Motif Breakfast Nook

Sweetheart Magazine Rack

This project is quite simple to make. One can be made in a couple of hours over a weekend or an evening. The actual time involved will be dependent on how many sweethearts you have. The decorative tole painting is optional. You may wish to stain this project or use paint and stencils; the option are many. Just stand back and get ready to take requests.

MATERIALS

1x12 white pine 8 linear feet
  2 pieces 11" x 13" ends
  2 pieces 9" x 16" sides
  1 piece 6¼" x 16" bottom
  1 piece 5" x 16" center or handle

HARDWARE AND MISCELLANEOUS

20 screws 1½" drywall type
20 wood plugs ½"
Carpenter's or Titebond glue
1 pint paint or stain

TOOLS REQUIRED

Circular saw
Saber saw
Drill with ½" countersink and
  ½" bit
Screwdriver
Router with rounding over bit

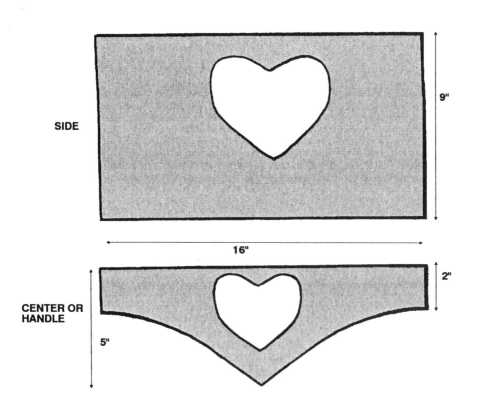

SIDE

9"

16"

CENTER OR HANDLE

5"

2"

INSTRUCTIONS

1. Measure and cut all wood pieces to size.

2. Draw the heart designs onto cardboard and cut to shape with a scissors.

3. Using the heart patterns, draw the designs onto the center, end and side boards. Feel free to use other designs such as tulips or diamonds or any shape you desire. You are not restricted to the sizes I used, although I do not recommend making the sizes any larger as this might tend to weaken the structure.

4. Drill countersunk screw holes into the two end boards. I suggest

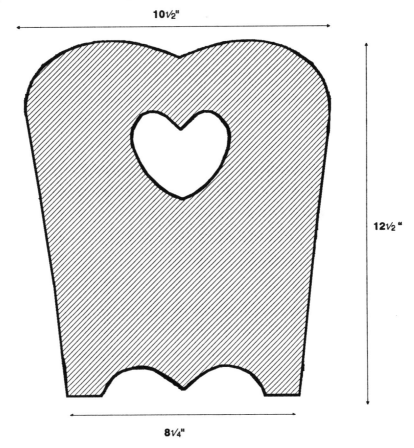

10½"

12½ "

8¼"

using three screws for the sides and two each for the bottom and center boards.

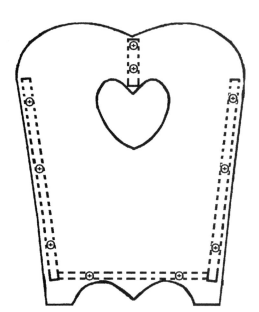

5. Using a router with a rounding over bit, rout the edges of the end boards, the tops of the center and side boards and the heart shapes of all boards.

6. Assemble the project using screws and glue.

7. Glue wood plugs in the screw holes and sand flush.

8. Sand all rough spots.

9. Stain or paint the project the color of your choice.

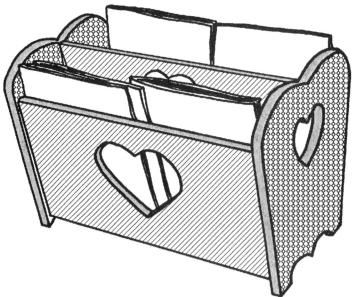

Blanket Chest

This is a straightforward and simple design that serves as both a blanket chest and a settle. Put it at the foot of your bed, and it's a place to sit as well as store towels, blankets, clothing, shoes and summer and winter special items. You can make it from cedar or pine, a hardwood or special hardwood plywood. At a very minimum you want to line it with cedar blocks that will keep out moths and other pests.

MATERIALS

Note: The front, back, sides, floor and lid are made by splining wood planks together to form the widths needed for the pieces. In some areas of the country you can purchase wood planks already splined up to 24" width.

3/4" white pine 12" x 36 linear feet
    1 piece 10¼" x 48" front
    1 piece 15" x 48" back
    1 piece 2" x 44¾" back brace
    2 pieces 18½" x 19⅜" sides
    2 pieces 2" x 18½" side braces
    1 piece 6" x 48" front bottom trim
    1 piece 18½" x 46½" floor
    2 pieces 2¼" x 16½" lid brace
    1 piece 1¼" x 47¾" lid trim

¼" pressed cedar board liner 27
        square feet
    1 piece 18½" x 46½" floor
    2 pieces 14" x 18½" sides
    1 piece 14" x 46" back
    1 piece 16" x 46" front
    1 piece 17" x 40" lid

HARDWARE AND MISCELLANEOUS

2 butt hinges 2" long brass
    1 tube panel adhesive (for cedar
        liner)
    Carpenter's or Titebond glue

30 screws 1½"
30 wood plugs ½"
40 biscuit splines No. 20
1 pint Danish oil (walnut)

TOOLS REQUIRED

Circular saw
Saber saw
Drill with ½" counter sink
Screwdriver
Router with ⅛" slot cutter and
    rounding over bit
Bar or pipe clamps 24"

INSTRUCTIONS

The chest is basically a box with two sides, back, floor, front and lid. Braces inside the back and side walls support the hinged lid. Cedar lining is attached with panel adhesive.

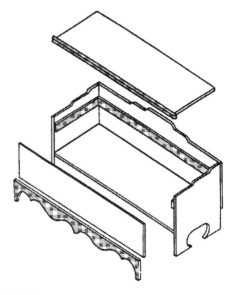

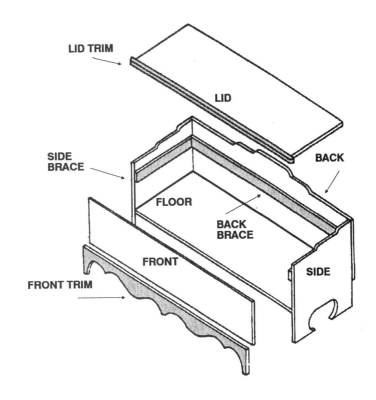

THE CHEST IS A VERY SIMPLE BOX

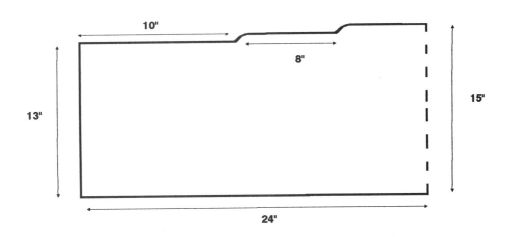

LEFT SIDE OF CHEST BACK; DOUBLE FOR CUTTING

1. Measure and cut all of the wood pieces. For those boards requiring splining, including the front pieces, cut the necessary board widths to meet the size requirements of the piece. Rout blind dados in the sides of these boards, insert biscuit splines and clamp the boards using bar or pipe clamps. Allow the glue to dry thoroughly.

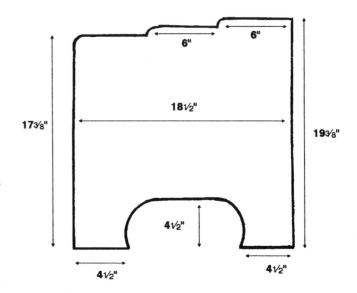

CHEST SIDE; MAKE TWO

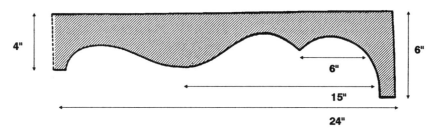

FRONT TRIM RIGHT SIDE PATTERN

2. Begin the assembly by attaching one side to the back. Butt the pieces together as shown. Use glue and countersunk screws. Glue and screw the floor to these two pieces. The bottom of the floor should be even with the lower edge of the back.

3. Add the remaining side and front, forming the basic chest.

4. Attach the side braces on the inside, flush with the top of the front. Attach the back brace so that it is flush with the tops of the side braces.

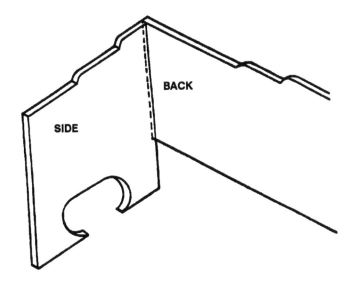

ATTACH THE BACK TO THE SIDE

5. Attach the lid trim and the lid braces to the lid.

6. Glue wood plugs into the countersunk screw holes and sand flush with the wood surface.

7. Measure and cut the cedar closet lining boards.

8. Attach the cedar lining inside the lid, sides, front, back and sides using panel adhesive. Note: If you use nails, be certain they are recessed.

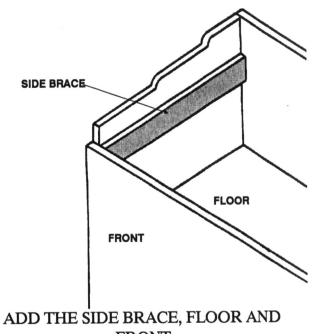

ADD THE SIDE BRACE, FLOOR AND FRONT

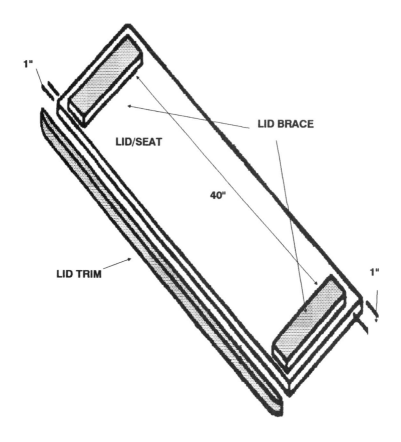

1"

LID BRACE

LID/SEAT

40"

LID TRIM

1"

LID ASSEMBLY

9. Attach the brass butt hinges to the lid assembly and attach this assembly to the chest.

10. Stain the chest the color of your choice and varnish it with a satin finish polyurethane.

11. This step is optional. If you wish to have an upholstered seating area, wrap some fabric around 1" foam padding and a piece of ¼" plywood, cut to fit the space on top of the lid, roughly 17½" x 46". It is not necessary to attach this assembly to the chest. Simply lay it on top of the lid so as the fabric ages, you can easily replace it.

12. Store all of your blankets and towels, stand back and pat yourself on the back for a job well done.

ADD A 1" PAD OF FOAM RUBBER AND COVER WITH FABRIC

NOTES AND CALCULATIONS

Early American Dry Sink

When this furniture was first made, it was designed to hold a wash basin, a pitcher of water and some soap. Usually there was a towel hanging from its side, and this is where the family washed up for dinner, or breakfast, after the harvest, etc. In today's world it serves a different purpose. In my case, it sits in the bedroom and holds photos of grandchildren, and it's where I put my change at night. This project is made from cherry and will look good anywhere you decide to put it. It's certain to get lots of compliments from onlookers.

MATERIALS

Note: This project is made from splined wood pieces that form the sides, top and back. The sizes shown are for the final assembled wood pieces. I recommend you use either red oak or cherry for the surface lumber.

1x8 cherry or red oak, 50 square feet

Splined pieces
  1 piece 18¾" x 37 ½" floor
  1 piece 28 ¼" x 37½" lower back
  2 pieces 19½" x 28¼" lower sides
  1 piece 20½" x 39" counter
  1 piece 18½" x 37¼" shelf
  1 piece 10" x 39" upper back
  2 pieces 11¼" x 22" upper sides

Regular cuts
  1 piece 7" x 40½" top
  1 piece 4" x 40½" front

Front section
  2 pieces 5½" x 28¼" front sides
  1 piece 3" x 28" upper strut
  1 piece 4¼" x 28" lower strut
  1 piece 3½" x 28¼" center divider
  4 pieces 2" x 18½" door stile
  4 pieces 2" x 13" door rail
  4 pieces ¾" x¾ "x 11" door rail molding

4 pieces ¾"x ¾" x 20½" door stile molding
2 pieces ¾" x ¾" x 18½" shelf support
2 pieces 2¾" x 21¼" lower side molding
1 piece 2¾" x 41" lower front molding
1 piece ¾" x ¾" x 39" back counter molding
2 pieces ¾" x ¾" x 20½" side counter molding

¼" cherry faced plywood
  2 pieces 9½" x 19" door panel

1x3 pine support section, 20 linear feet
  2 pieces 2½" x 37½" front
  2 pieces 2½" x 36" back
  4 pieces 2½" x 18" sides

HARDWARE AND MISCELLANEOUS

4 hinges butt type   2"
2 knobs white porcelain
2 magnetic stays
100 screws 1½" drywall type
100 cherry wood plugs ½"
Carpenter's or Titebond glue
1 quart clear Danish oil

TOOLS REQUIRED

Drill with ½" countersink bit
Screwdriver
Table saw
Belt or pad sander
Router with cove bit and ¼" slot
  cutter
Router table and rabbet bit
Biscuit joiner (optional)
Pipe clamps 4 feet
Carpenter's square

INSTRUCTIONS

Basic construction notes: This project consists of three splined walls (the back and two sides), a front section with two frame and panel doors, a splined counter, floor and shelf. The walls are assembled around two rectangular frames, one at the bottom and one at the top. The top part consists of two splined curved sides, a curved front and top board and one splined, straight back piece.

1. Measure and cut all of the wood pieces to make the splined sections or assemblies. You can opt to use a router to cut spline dados in the wood edges or use a biscuit joiner for that purpose. Another option is the use of a table saw to cut dados for the splines. Join the boards and clamp and glue and allow to dry overnight. Make certain that there is no warp in the boards when clamped. Also see to it that the board edges are flush where they are joined.

2. Measure and cut to size all remaining wood pieces except for the front boards. Sand the boards to remove any rough edges.

3. Assemble the pine frames as shown. Use glue and at least two screws in each corner. I recommend that you also cut glue blocks to stabilize the corners of the frames and make certain they are square.

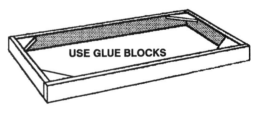

USE GLUE BLOCKS

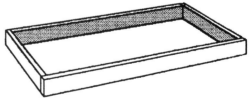

TOP AND BOTTOM FRAMES

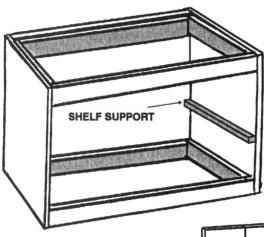

SHELF SUPPORT

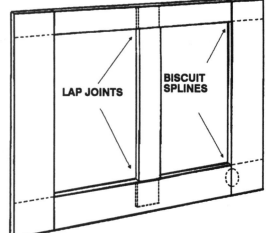

LAP JOINTS

BISCUIT SPLINES

4. Attach the sides and backs to the frames using glue and screws that have been countersunk. The sides will overlap the edges of the back piece.

5. Attach the shelf supports to the sides about in the center of the cabinet or wherever you want it. Attach the floor and shelf using screws and

TOP ASSEMBLY

BASE WITH TOP

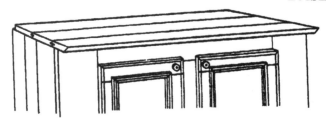

TOP WITH BACK

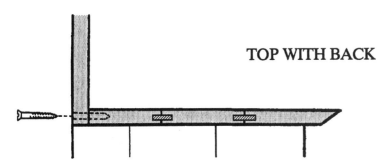

glue. Glue wood plugs into the countersunk holes and sand flush. Do this now, as later it will be difficult to perform.

6. The boards for the front frame can be assembled in one of two ways. You can cut lap joints for the center and top and bottom boards or you can opt to use biscuit splines or regular splines for that purpose. If you opt to use lap joints, increase the length of the top and bottom boards accordingly. Measure and cut all of the front boards.

7. Assemble the front frame and attach it to the front of the cabinet using screws and glue. Glue wood plugs into the countersunk screw holes and sand flush.

8. Attach the upper back board to the counter as shown.

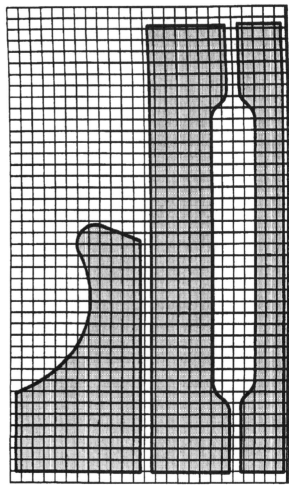

PATTERNS FOR UPPER PIECES ONE
SQUARE = 1"

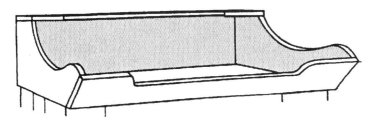

FINISHED TOP

DOOR ASSEMBLY

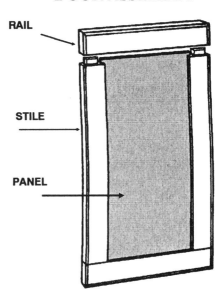

Attach this assembly to the top of the cabinet. Glue wood plugs in place and sand flush.

9. Attach the upper side pieces to the upper back and counter. Add the top and front. Again tap wood plugs into place in the countersunk screw holes and sand flush.

10. Assemble the parts for the panel and frame doors and assemble each door. The stiles and rails are connected with blind splines or biscuit splines. Do not glue the panel in place. It should float in the dado. Glue the splined areas and clamp the pieces securely.

11. Rout the edges of the front of the doors with a cove bit.

12. Rout the molding for the facing of the doors as shown. Cut the molding to size and glue to the inside of the door frame and not to the facing. It is unlikely that you will find store-bought moldings made from cherry, so this is a step that you must perform with a router and a router table. You need to cut a ½" rabbet on one side and a cove cut on the other. If you are really ambitious, you can cut a smaller cove on the other side as shown, or opt to leave it plain as the drawing shows.

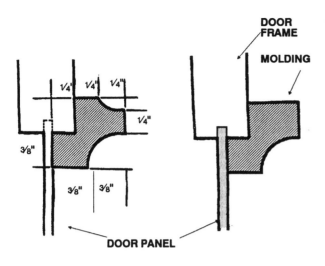

DOOR FRAME

MOLDING

¼" ¼" ¼"

¼"

³⁄₈"

³⁄₈" ³⁄₈"

DOOR PANEL

13. Attach the doors to the front using brass butt hinges. I used small white porcelain knobs for door handles. Attach the magnetic stays on the inside so the doors stay shut.

14. Attach the 2¾" molding around the bottom front and sides. Use screws and glue and fill the recessed screw holes with wood plugs and glue. Sand flush. Attach the ¾" square molding to the inside of the sides, front and back of the counter area, use finishing nails and glue for this purpose. Recess the nail heads and fill the holes with wood filler.

FINISHING THE PROJECT

I used a walnut colored Danish oil stain and applied about three coats. This gave the cherry a rich dark color that makes it an outstanding piece of furniture. If you want more of the cherry look use a clear Danish oil. Remember though, each successive coat will turn the wood darker.

Stand back and admire your beautiful new furniture piece. Congratulations.

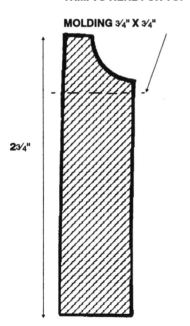

TRIM TO HERE FOR TOP

MOLDING ¾" X ¾"

2¾"

FRONT AND SIDE MOLDING

NOTES AND CALCULATIONS

Lap Desk

This project is a holdover from days long ago when people needed a writing surface and perhaps couldn't afford an upright desk. A lap desk is something you can use on your lap while at home sitting in a chair or sofa or on the floor, when taking a long car trip or maybe just sitting on the edge of your bed. You can store papers, pen and ink and pencils, along with rulers and other standard desk paraphernalia, inside of it. Best of all, this project can be done in an evening in the workshop.

MATERIALS

1x18 splined white pine 7 board feet
   1 piece 14¼" x 17¾" lid
   1 piece 16½" square bottom
   2 pieces 4" x 18" sides
   1 piece 4" x 16½" back
   1 piece 3½" x 17¾" top back
   1 piece 2" x 16½" front
   1 piece 1" x 17¾" lid lip
   1 piece 1" x 16½" inside divider

HARDWARE AND MISCELLANEOUS

Carpenter's or Titebond glue
24 screws 1½" drywall type
24 wood plugs ½"
2 hinges 2" brass
1 pint paint or stain of your choice

TOOLS REQUIRED

Drill with countersink bit
Screwdriver
Pipe clamps
Circular saw
Router with rounding over bit
  (optional)
Pad or belt sander

INSTRUCTIONS

1. Measure and cut all of the wood pieces, except the lid and the top back, to the sizes specified. Note the dimensions of the drawing of the side piece.

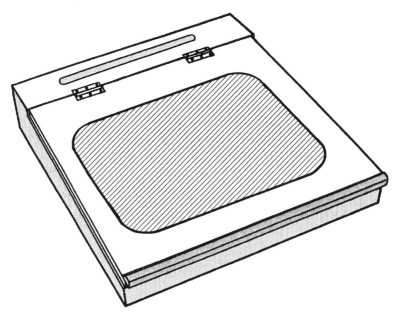

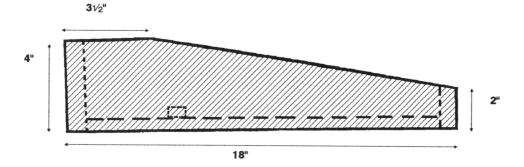

3½"

4"

18"

2"

SIDE; MAKE TWO

2. Begin the assembly by putting the sides, front, back and bottom boards together first. I suggest you glue these up and hold in place with pipe clamps. Predrill the screw holes and attach the screws to hold all of the pieces together and then remove the pipe clamps.

3. Place the inside divider inside so that you can keep pens and pencils separated from the paper. Place this about 6 or so inches

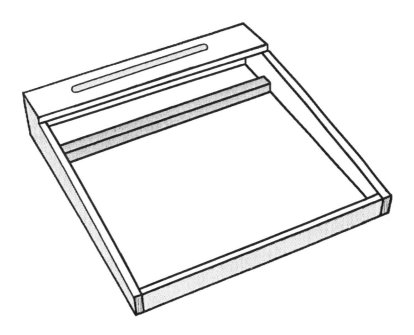

from the back. Attach it to the bottom board using two screws and glue. Fill the screw holes with wood plugs and sand them flush.

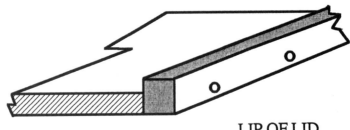

LIP OF LID

4. Measure and cut the lid and the top back. The edge where they meet in the assembly should be cut at about a 10 degree angle so that they fit flush and compensate for the tilt of the lid. I'm usually a little off when doing this kind of stuff and "good enough" is my usual attitude. If you're an "A type" and a stickler for angles and precision, double check the tilt and the angle.

5. Using a router with a rounding over bit, rout both sides of one edge of the lip board. Attach it to the lid board with the rounding side up.

6. With a rounding over bit, rout the sides of the lid and the sides and back of the top back.

7. Attach the top back using screws and glue. Glue wood plugs into all of the screw holes and sand flush. Attach the lid using 2" brass hinges.

8. Stain or paint the project the color of your choice. You could also use stencils or transfer patterns. Seal the project with a good varnish.

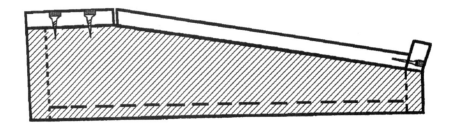

Deacon's Bench and Chest Combination

This project will look good anywhere. It is that perfect project for not only sitting on but also for storing winter's blankets. You could also use it as a hope chest or use it in the children's room to store toys and things. However you decide to use it, it will be a family heirloom to be cherished and passed along.

MATERIALS

Note: The sides, front, floor, back, seat and upper back are all made from splined boards. It will be necessary to make up these panels and then cut to size to finish this project. You may opt to use a hardwood plywood instead and simply cover the veneer edges with solid wood strips.

1x4 white pine 48 linear feet
    1 piece 3" x 48" base front
    1 piece 3" x 46½" base back
    2 pieces 3" x 22" base sides
    2 pieces 3" x 48" front and back top inner frame
    2 pieces 3" x 22¾ " sides top inner frame
    1 piece 21¼" x 46½" splined floor
    8 pieces 3" x 3" triangular glue blocks
    4 pieces ¾" square and 12" long glue strips

1x8 red oak lumber 72 linear feet

Splined boards
    1 piece 16" x 49½" front
    1 piece 16" x 48" back
    2 pieces 16" x 23½" sides
    1 piece 18" x 46" upper back
    1 piece 17" x 41" seat/lid

Solid lumber
    2 pieces 3" x 50½" front top and bottom facing
    2 pieces 3" x 49½" back top and bottom facing
    4 pieces 3" x 24¼" side top and bottom facing
    4 pieces 3" x 10" corner facing
    4 pieces 2¼" x 10" corner facing
    2 pieces 5" x 25" end seat boards
    1 piece 7" x 41" back seat board
    2 pieces 3" x 46" mitered back facing top and bottom boards
    2 pieces 3" x 19" mitered back facing side boards
    1 piece 1" x 41" upper back top trim
    1 piece 1" x 41" seat front trim board
    2 pieces 2" x 19½" armrest base
    2 pieces 2" x 20" armrest top
    2 pieces 8" x 19" armrest center

1x4 walnut lumber 12 linear feet ripped to ¾" square strips and cut to size for molding (optional).

    4 pieces top and bottom molding for front and back ¾"
    4 pieces top and bottom side molding
    4 pieces side molding seat back
    4 pieces top and bottom seat back molding

HARDWARE AND MISCELLANEOUS

100 biscuit splines medium
100 screws 1½" drywall type
100 wood plugs ½"
Carpenter's or Titebond glue
2 hinges brass 3"
1 quart walnut Danish oil

TOOLS REQUIRED

Circular saw or table saw
Saber saw
Biscuit joiner
Router with cove and rounding
  over bit
Drill with ½" bit and countersink
Screwdriver
Belt or pad sander

INSTRUCTIONS

1. Measure and cut all of the wood pieces forming the splined boards. Glue and clamp all boards and allow to dry at least 24 hours.

2. Measure and cut the pine boards forming the base frame and the inner frame. Attach these boards as shown using screws and glue. Attach the glue blocks in the corners ¾" from the edge of the top. Attach wood glue strips under the floor boards and use screws and glue to hold the assembly together.

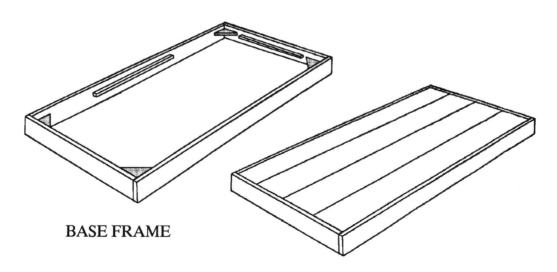

BASE FRAME

BASE AND FLOOR

3. Attach the side, front and back splined sections covering the base and forming a box. Attach the inner frame on the inside of the assembly on top of glue blocks glued into the corners of the wood box. This must be flush with the top of the side, back and front splined sections.

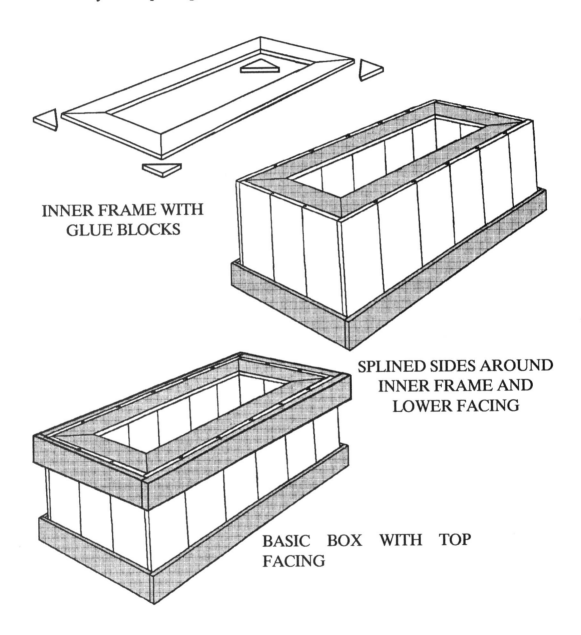

INNER FRAME WITH
GLUE BLOCKS

SPLINED SIDES AROUND
INNER FRAME AND
LOWER FACING

BASIC BOX WITH TOP
FACING

4. Attach the side front and back facing boards to the box from the above step. Use screws that are countersunk and glue. Fill the screw holes with wood plugs and sand flush.

5. Attach the side facing boards, forming 3" corners. Sand the wood plugs flush.

6. Measure and cut the seat side and back boards. Attach them as shown using screws and glue. Again fill the holes with wood plugs and sand flush.

7. Assemble the seat board as shown. Attach a 1" wood strip along the front of the splined seat section covering the end grain of the boards. For insurance purposes, attach two support

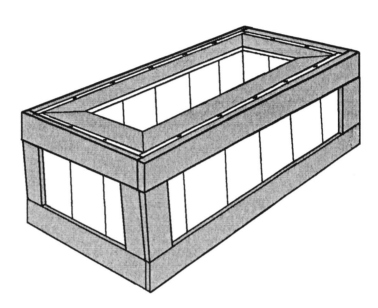

SEAT WITH TOP
BOTTOM AND
CORNER FACINGS

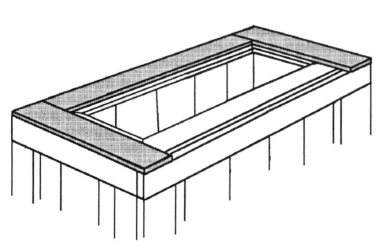

boards to the bottom of the splined seat section. Make certain the placement does not interfere with the front or back boards the seat must fit on.

8. Attach the seat using two 3" brass hinges.

9. Using a router with a cove bit, rout the edge of the top on all four sides.

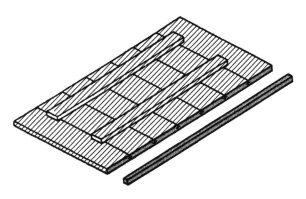

SEAT WITH FRONT TRIM BOARD

10. Rout the outside edge of the board to be used for the back rest facing with a cove bit. Measure and cut the side, top and bottom pieces with miter cuts on the ends as shown.

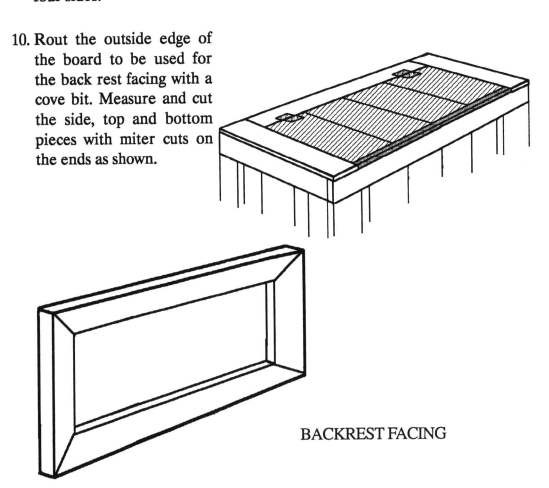

BACKREST FACING

11. In the center of the splined back rest, cut a heart design as shown. The design that I used was about 7" wide and 6" tall. You can use any cutout you prefer, from hearts to tulips. Drill a starter hole and cut the design to size using a sabre saw. Rout this design on both sides with a router and a rounding over bit.

12. Attach the backrest facing boards onto the back using screws and glue. Make certain that the routed side is facing outward. Fill the screw holes with wood plugs and sand smooth.

13. Assemble the armrest as shown.

14. Stain the color of your choice.

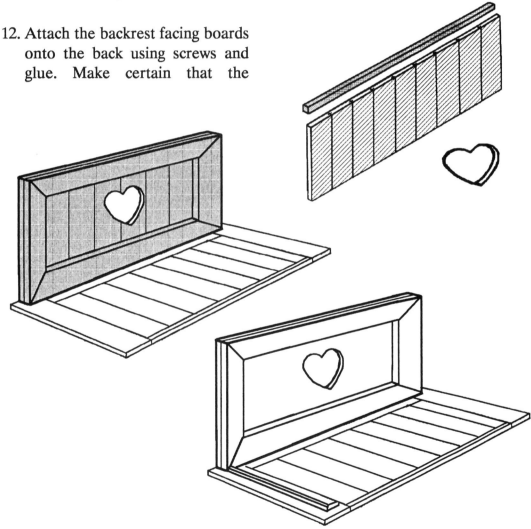

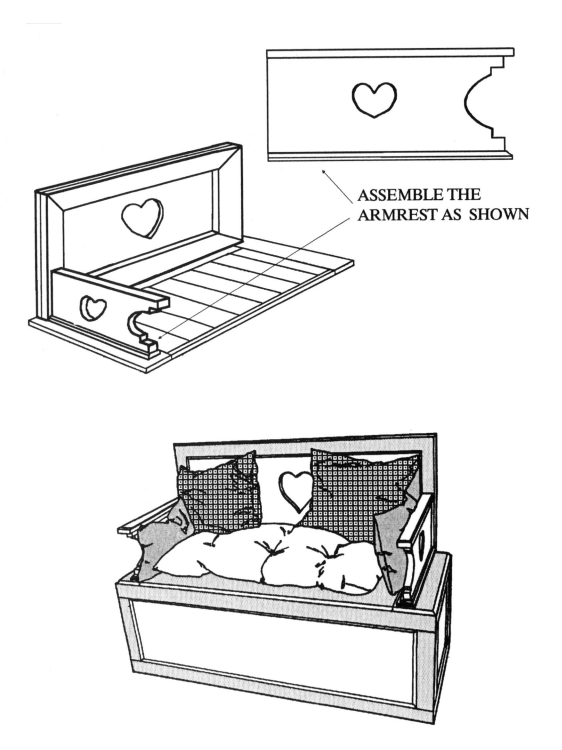

ASSEMBLE THE
ARMREST AS SHOWN

Tulip Motif Breakfast Nook

This project takes up just a little space and it is guaranteed to be a conversation piece when you finish making it. Its construction is so simple you will be amazed at how fast you can put it all together. Allow yourself a couple of weekends to make it. Start with the benches first and then the table. I finished this one with a blue aquamarine finish and then coated it with varnish.

MATERIALS

Benches (each)

1x18 splined pine 20 linear feet
    1 piece 17½" x 48" backrest
    1 piece 18" x 48" seat
    2 pieces 18" x 35" sides
    2 pieces 3" x 48" seat support front
       and back
    2 pieces 3" x 15½" seat support
       inner sides
    2 pieces 3" x 13¼" back side
       support
    2 pieces 3" x 13¼" front side
       support
    4 pieces 2" x 2" glue blocks
    4 pieces 3" x 3" corner glue blocks
    2 pieces ½" x ⅛" x 13" tulip backing
       strips
    2 pieces ½" x ⅛" x 8½" tulip
       backing strips

2x4 white pine 30"
    18 pieces ¼" x 1½" x 8" side
       decorator pieces

Table

1x18 splined pine 25 linear feet
    2 pieces 3" x 28½" leg/table top
       supports
    1 piece (splined) 34" x 60" table top
    2 pieces 2" x 34" table top ends
    2 pieces 2½" x 34" bottom table top
       ends
    2 pieces 2" x 59" bottom table top
       sides
    2 pieces 3" x 59" side molding
    2 pieces 3" x 30" end molding
    2 pieces 10" x 29" legs
    4 pieces 3" x 7" leg inner feet
    4 pieces 3" x 24" leg out side feet

2x4 white pine 60"
    2 pieces 2¼" x 9" leg support ends
    2 pieces 1¼" x 42" leg support
       centers
    16 pieces ⅛" x 1½" x 2½" leg center
       support decorative heart cutout
       pieces

HARDWARE AND MISCELLANEOUS

2 pieces ½" x 4" wood dowel
Carpenter's or Titebond glue
100 wood screws 1½" drywall type
100 wood plugs ½" pine
1 quart stain of your choice
1 quart varnish of your choice
Box medium biscuit splines
  (optional)
30 wire brads ½"

TOOLS REQUIRED

Drill with ½" bit and countersink
Screwdriver
Saber saw
Circular saw
Router with cove, rounding over
    bit and ⅛" slot cutter
Band saw
Pad or belt sander
Pipe clamps

INSTRUCTIONS (table)

Note: 1x18 splined white pine is exactly ¾" x 18" and is not measured the same as conventional lumber. If there is none at your local lumber dealer, you will have to spline narrower boards to create the ones called for in the materials list.

1. Measure and cut the wood pieces per the materials list.

2. Using a copying machine, enlarge the other patterns to full size. Trace onto the wood and cut to the shapes specified.

3. Start with the center piece called the leg supports. This unit is comprised of the center decorative tulip pieces, two end pieces cut from 2x4s and two strips cut from a 2x4, one on top and the other

on the bottom. The decorative tulip pieces are first cut to shape from a 2½" long piece of 2x4 and then sliced to a width of ⅛". Cut the pieces to size.

4. Cut a dado ⅛" wide and ¼" deep into the center of the top and bottom strips. Assemble the leg

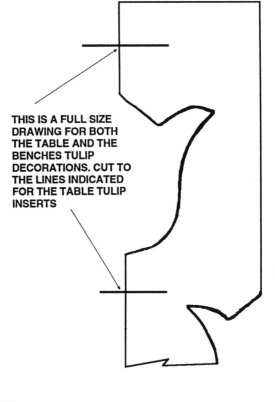

THIS IS A FULL SIZE DRAWING FOR BOTH THE TABLE AND THE BENCHES TULIP DECORATIONS. CUT TO THE LINES INDICATED FOR THE TABLE TULIP INSERTS

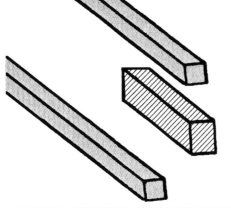

YOU FORM A SANDWICH, LAMINATING THE BOARDS

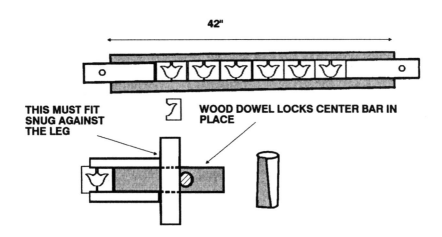

42"

THIS MUST FIT SNUG AGAINST THE LEG

WOOD DOWEL LOCKS CENTER BAR IN PLACE

support unit by sandwiching the decorative tulip pieces and the end pieces between the top and bottom pieces. Glue and clamp.

5. Trace the designs for the leg feet onto wood and cut to shape. You will need two pieces for the inner feet and two outside pieces that sandwich the leg forming the laminated foot. prepare the assembly using countersunk screws and glue. Cover the screw heads with wood plugs and sand flush.

6. Attach the legs to the leg support by placing the leg support through the center cutout in the legs. Tap a 4" length of ½" wood dowel into the hole. Note it may be necessary to sand one side of the dowel flat, at a slight

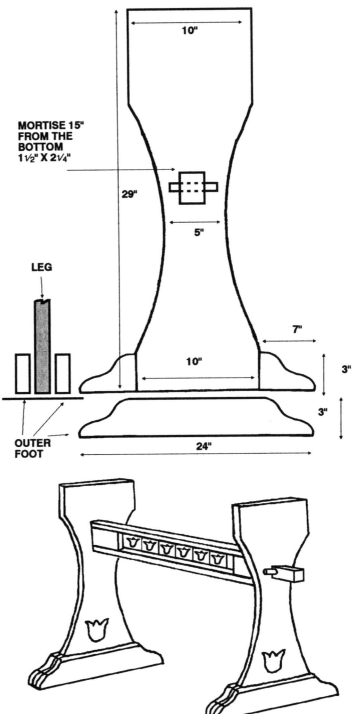

MORTISE 15"
FROM THE
BOTTOM
1½" X 2¼"

29"

10"

5"

7"

3"

3"

10"

24"

LEG

OUTER
FOOT

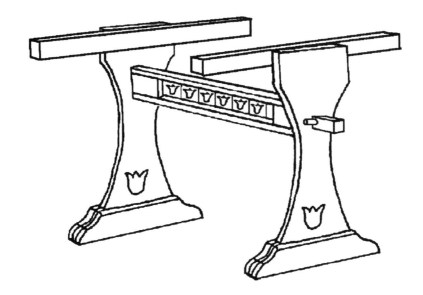

angle to make the fit snug. Glue the wood dowel in place.

7. Attach the leg/table top supports to the top of the legs as shown. Make certain the supports are centered and flush with the tops of the legs. Attach using glue and screws.

8. The next step is to assemble the table top and supports. The table consists of two 16" wide boards splined together and then capped at the end with two other boards to cover the end grain. Next a second layer of wood is placed around the lower sides with molding on the inside of that. This gives the appearance of a thick table top. Spline the center

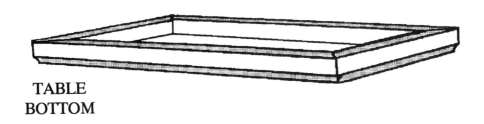

**TABLE
BOTTOM**

TABLE TOP

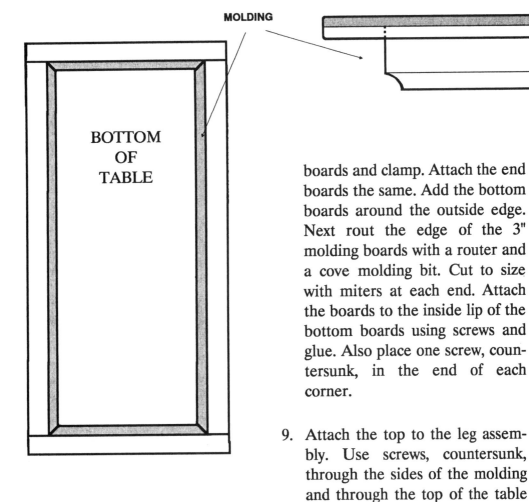

MOLDING

**BOTTOM
OF
TABLE**

boards and clamp. Attach the end boards the same. Add the bottom boards around the outside edge. Next rout the edge of the 3" molding boards with a router and a cove molding bit. Cut to size with miters at each end. Attach the boards to the inside lip of the bottom boards using screws and glue. Also place one screw, countersunk, in the end of each corner.

9. Attach the top to the leg assembly. Use screws, countersunk, through the sides of the molding and through the top of the table surface. Make certain the

assembly is centered before you attempt this. Fill the screw holes with wood plugs and sand flush.

INSTRUCTIONS (Benches)

1. Measure and cut the wood pieces forming the benches.

2. Drill a starter hole in the side pieces and cut the rectangular shape. Using a router with a rounding over bit, rout the outside edge of the sides on all sides. Rout the inside of the rectangular cutout with a ½" rabbet bit, creating a ½" dado or groove.

3. Measure and cut the tulip pieces from the 2x4 stock. This is done by first cutting the tulip half and then slicing the stock to a thickness of ⅛". Sand these pieces to remove all rough edges. Measure and cut the tulip backing strips.

4. Attach the tulip cut outs to the inside of the rectangular cut out of the sides using glue and back with the backing strips. Reverse every other tulip strip to get the full

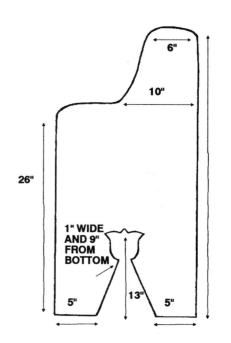

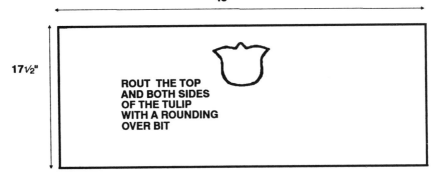

48"

17½"

ROUT THE TOP
AND BOTH SIDES
OF THE TULIP
WITH A ROUNDING
OVER BIT

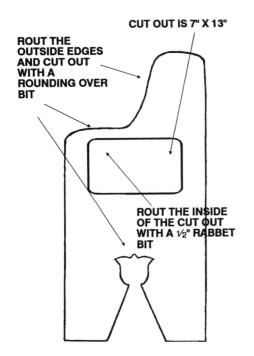

CUT OUT IS 7" X 13"

ROUT THE
OUTSIDE EDGES
AND CUT OUT
WITH A
ROUNDING OVER
BIT

ROUT THE INSIDE
OF THE CUT OUT
WITH A ½" RABBET
BIT

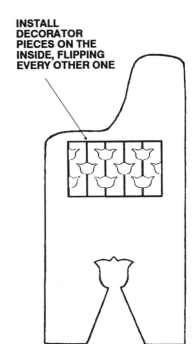

INSTALL
DECORATOR
PIECES ON THE
INSIDE, FLIPPING
EVERY OTHER ONE

tulip shape. Hold in place with small ½" wire brads.

5. Build the seat support by attaching the front and back pieces to the sides and attaching glue blocks in the corners. Use screws

and glue, fill the screw holes with wood plugs and sand flush.

6. Attach the front and the back side supports to the bottom of the seat support. Use small 2" glue blocks for this purpose. Use

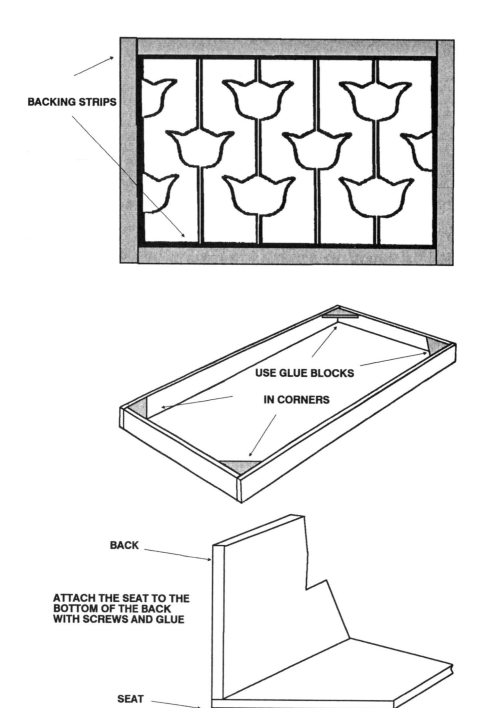

BACKING STRIPS

USE GLUE BLOCKS

IN CORNERS

BACK

**ATTACH THE SEAT TO THE
BOTTOM OF THE BACK
WITH SCREWS AND GLUE**

SEAT

SCREW

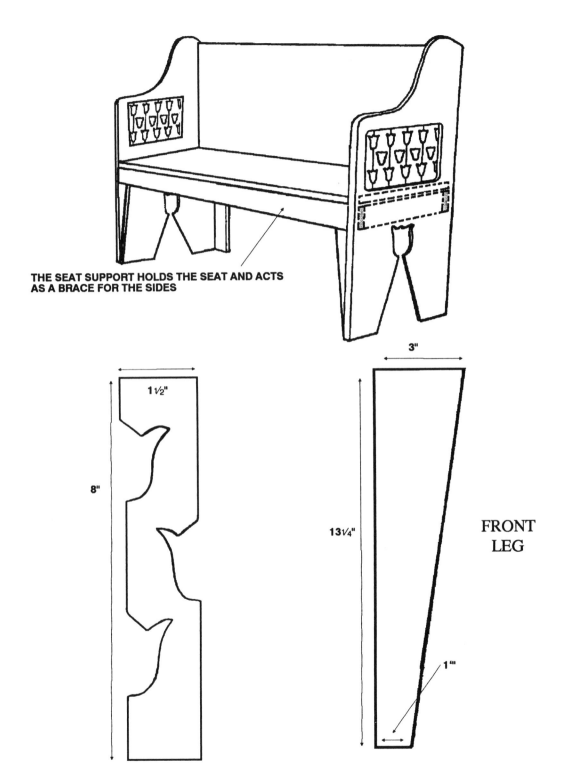

THE SEAT SUPPORT HOLDS THE SEAT AND ACTS AS A BRACE FOR THE SIDES

1½"

8"

3"

13¼"

FRONT
LEG

1'''

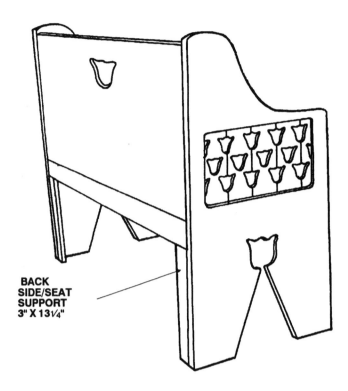

**BACK
SIDE/SEAT
SUPPORT
3" X 13¼"**

screws from the inside, through the glue blocks and into the supports. Attach this assembly so that it is flush with the back of the sides. Use glue and attach with screws through the inside of the seat support and into the sides. Make certain that the rounded edge of the sides is facing outward.

7. Rout the top of the seat back and the tulip cutout with a router and a rounding over bit. Rout the front lip of the seat the same. Glue the back edge of the seat to the bottom edge of the back and use countersunk screws. Attach this assembly to the seat support and flush with the back inside of the sides. Again countersink screws, glue, fill the holes with wood plugs and sand flush.

FINISHING THE PROJECTS

I used an oil-based blue aquamarine stain on top of a sander sealer finish. When working with pine, it is necessary to add a sander sealer finish to get an even staining effect. Pine will normally take stain quite unevenly and the results are never certain so the sander sealer is a must. Next I used an oil-based varnish and rubbed the surface with steel wool, then applied a second coat. After the surface was dried I added some lemon oil finish. I never use wax on furniture as it builds up in time and dulls the surface and only acts as a dust collector.

NOTES AND CALCULATIONS

Forever Calendar Clock

There are many different ways to make a calendar clock. I used a clock face from some cross-stitched material. You can use wood or regular clock faces that can be purchased from the same store where you buy the clock movement. This is also a project that could be tole-painted, and you could have small wood month plaques that could be used each month. In any event, you will have a nice project to show off over your mantel.

MATERIALS

1x12 clear pine 3 linear feet
    2 pieces 3" x 16½" sides
    2 pieces 3" x 12½" top and
    bottom
    1 piece 4 ⅛" x 12½ " top trim

¼" hardwood plywood 1½ board feet
    1 piece 11 ½" x 15½ " clock face
    28 pieces 3" x 3" calendar months
    (optional)

½" corner molding 5 linear feet
    2 piece ½" x ½" x 15 ⅛" side
    molding
    2 pieces ½" x ½" x 11" top and
    bottom molding
Note: You can make your own
molding from scrap pine.

HARDWARE AND MISCELLANEOUS

1 quartz battery operated clock
    movement
8 wood screws 1 ½"
8 wood plugs ½"
1 piece aida cloth ivory colored
    11" x 15" face (optional)
28 pieces Aida cloth ivory colored
    4" x 4" calendar months (optional)
Navy embroidery floss (optional)
 strip Velcro 36" for calendar
    backing (optional)
Several small containers acrylic
    enamel (optional)
Small container clear varnish
Small container stain of your
    choice
Carpenter's wood glue
10 wire brads ¾"
Small container wood filler
Medium grit sandpaper

TOOLS REQUIRED

Circular saw
Drill with ½" countersink bit and
    ½" wood bit
Screwdriver
Hammer with nail set
Web clamp
Sewing machine (optional)
Tapestry needle /thread(optional)

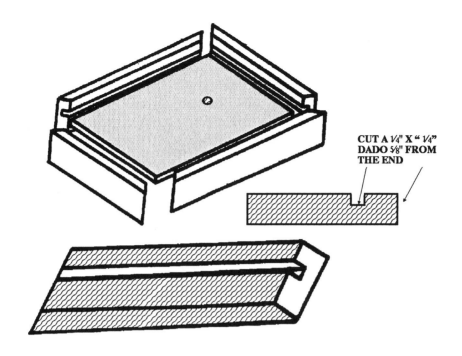

CUT A ¼" X " ¼"
DADO ⅝" FROM
THE END

CLOCK MAIN COMPONENTS

1 SQUARE = 1 INCH

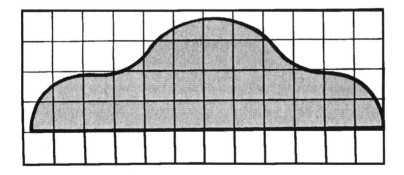

INSTRUCTIONS

1. Measure and cut the pieces forming the clock sides, top, bottom

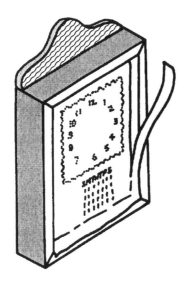

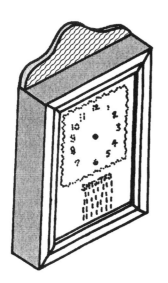

and face. The ends are cut at a 45 degree miter. You can set your circular saw to this angle and make the cuts. I suggest you double check the angle of the saw blade with a miter square.

2. Cut a ¼" wide dado, ¼" deep into the inside of the clock sides, top and bottom. Cut this dado ⅝" from the face edge of the boards. I suggest you do this before cutting the boards. You can use a dado head on your saw or make multiple passes with a regular saw blade to do this step.

3. Assemble the clock sides, top, bottom and face as shown. Glue the edges of the boards and clamp with a web clamp. Do not glue the face board in place, it should float in the dado slots.

4. Drill countersunk screw holes into the edges of the mitered top and bottom boards and insert 1½" screws. Fill the holes with wood plugs and glue and sand flush.

5. Measure and cut the top trim and sand it smooth. Attach it so that it is flush with the back of the top board of the clock with screws and glue.

6. It is at this juncture you must decide to use the needlepoint face, paint the face or use a store-bought face instead. If you opt for a painted face, you will need a quantity of different colored acrylic paints and an artist's fine-tipped paint brush.

MAKING THE FACE & CALENDAR MONTHS

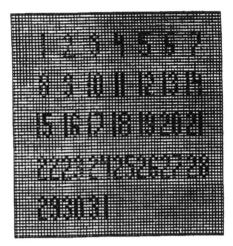

MONTH FORMAT

1. Whether you opt for a painted or cross-stitched face, the pattern layout is the same. You can follow the graph design on the small squares of the 14 count Aida cloth. One square of the cloth equals one square of the final design. I suggest you enlarge these designs to the face size using a copying machine.

2. You will need to make 21 calendar plaques to cover all of the month possibilities, 7 with 28 days, 7 with 30 days and 7 with 31 days, each starting on a different day of the week.

3. Attach the individual calendar plaques using Velcro glued to the front of the face and backs of the plaques.

4. If you opted for the cross-stitch, attach it to the face (do not use glue) and cut off the trim. Hold the cross-stitch in place with corner molding strips cut as listed. This allows you to remove the cloth at a later date for dry cleaning. Attach the molding strips with ¾" brads, recessing the nail holes and filling with wood filler.

5. Drill a ½" hole into the face to accommodate the clock main shaft. You should double check the diameter needed for this purpose. Most are ½".

6. Finish the clock with the stain and varnish of your choice.

7. Attach the clock movement and hands and go hang it in your favorite place in the house or wherever you wish it to be.

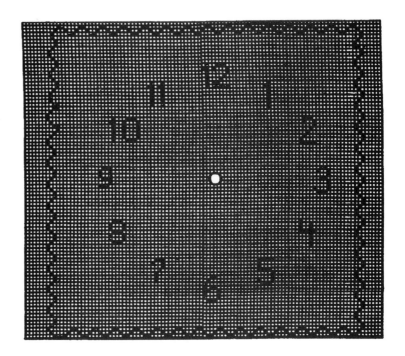

CLOCK FACE

CLOCK MONTH FACING

Country Modern Grandfather Clock

When you listen to the gonging sound of Father Time emanating from this unique clock, you get a warm, fuzzy feeling of comfort and security. I don't know why, but that's the feeling I get every time I listen to it. The works in this clock can play three different tunes. It chimes on the quarter hour, half hour and on the hour, plus it gongs the time of day. The important thing is this is a great looking project and it is very simple to make.

MATERIALS

Any hardwood lumber will do fine for this clock. Due to the delicate lines and the slender rails and framing, I would not use any softwood as it might not hold up to the stress. Honduras mahogany is the wood I chose, but walnut or cherry are also good choices. I would not use oak as it, like ash, tends to chip and splinter when making lots of dado cuts and this project requires a bunch of those kinds of cuts. Pecan or butternut are good, maybe teak, but that's expensive wood. You could use luan mahogany but it contains silica and chews up tool bits. Maple, padouk, elm, African mahogany and beech are other good choices. If you really want to spiffy it up and drop some dollars, use rosewood, bubinga or purpleheart.

Before you do anything, decide on the clock works you want to use and modify my instructions where needed to accommodate the works of your choice. I have listed names of companies that sell clock mechanisms at the end of this chapter.

1x4 hardwood lumber 30 linear feet
   8 pieces 1½" x 68" sides
   4 pieces 1½" x 14¼" front/back top and bottom
   4 pieces 1½" x 8" sides top and bottom
   2 pieces 1½" x 9¾" front/back vertical support
   2 pieces 1½" x 5½" sides vertical support
   60 linear feet ¼" x ¼" trim pieces

1x8 hardwood lumber 4 linear feet
   2 pieces 7" x 12¼" top and bottom supports
   1 piece 6½" x 12" clockworks shelf
   1 piece 2" x 11" clockworks support
   2 pieces 2" x 3" clockwork support legs
   2 pieces ½" x 6¾" clockworks shelf support

2x10 hardwood lumber 4 linear feet
   1 piece 9" x 15" routed to shape top crown
   1 piece 9" x 15" routed to shape bottom foot
   1 piece 10" x 16" routed to shape extra base/bottom

½" veneer core plywood 6 board feet
   1 piece 10¾" 53½" lower back
   1 piece 10¾" x 10¾" upper back

1/8" glass or scratch resistant acrylic
- 1 piece 10¾"x 53½" front door lower section
- 1 piece 10¾" x 10¾" front door upper section
- 2 pieces 5½" x 10¾" sides upper section
- 2 pieces 5½" 53½" sides lower section

HARDWARE AND MISCELLANEOUS

- 2 knife hinges about 2" long
- 1 knob brass
- 1 magnetic latch
- 1 piece acrylic sheet ¼" 11" x 11" clock face
- 20 screws 1½" drywall type
- 15 screws ⅝"
- 30 wood plugs ½" matching hardwood
- Carpenter's or Titebond wood glue
- 1 pint clear Danish oil
- Box wire brads ⅝"

TOOLS REQUIRED

Circular saw
Router with ½" rabbeting bit, cove and roman ogee bits
Screwdriver
Pad sander
Miter clamps
Wood clamps
Hammer

Chisel ½"
Back saw and miter box
Drill with ½" and countersink bits

INSTRUCTIONS

This project is basically one of making four frames, attaching three of them to a top and bottom block and hanging one of them in the front for a door. It's really that simple but it is

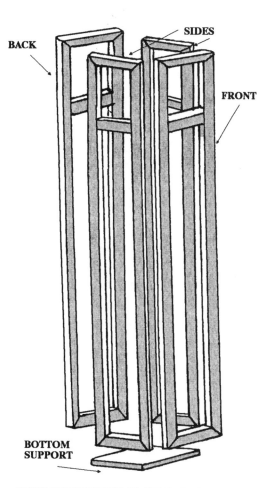

me consuming and we want to move carefully step by step.

1. Measure and cut the frame pieces 1½" wide.

2. Miter cut the ends of the pieces at a 45 degree angle. This cut must be a true miter because if you are off by as little as ¹⁄₁₆" at one end you will wind up being off ¼" over all.

3. Assemble the sides and the front and back minus the vertical supports. Cut a saw kerf in the center of the mitered ends as shown and insert a small wood spline. You make these splines by slicing pieces of matching hardwood the width of the blade and then cutting to fit the slot. Glue and clamp these assemblies. When dry, cut off the excess spline and sand flush.

4. Starting with the sides, cut a ¼" deep and ½"

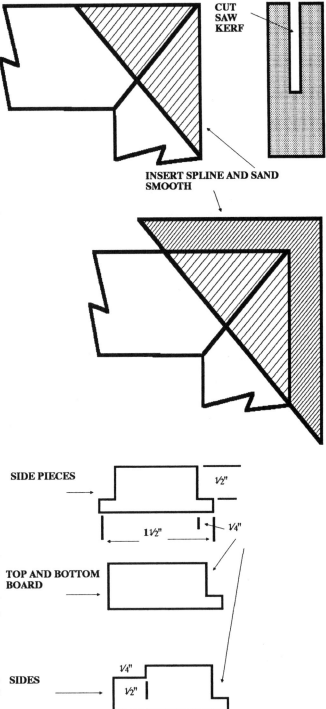

CUT SAW KERF

INSERT SPLINE AND SAND SMOOTH

SIDE PIECES

½"

1½"

¼"

TOP AND BOTTOM BOARD

SIDES

¼"

½"

wide dado in the outside edge as shown, not the top or bottom. You can use a router or a saw for this application. Using a router with a ½" rabbeting bit, rout the inside area on all four sides ½" deep and ¼" wide as shown. Using a chisel, square the corners.

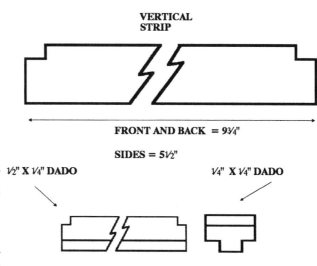

VERTICAL
STRIP

FRONT AND BACK = 9¾"

SIDES = 5½"

½" X ¼" DADO

¼" X ¼" DADO

5. Rout the inside and outside edges of the back and front frames with a router and a ½" rabbeting bit. Rout a dado ¼" wide and ½" deep as shown. Square the corners of the inside cut with a chisel.

6. Measure and cut the wood pieces forming the vertical strips. Rout the ends of the boards with a rabbeting bit creating a ¼" deep and wide dado. On the opposite side of the boards rout a ¼" wide and ½" deep dado as shown.

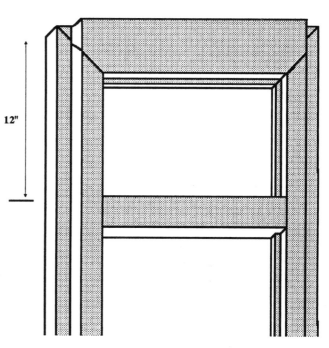

12"

7. Glue the vertical strips in place on the frames starting exactly 12" from the top of the frame. Attach the strips using ⅝" screws from the inside through the strip and into the frame. Cover the holes with wood plugs and sand flush. Note:

you don't have much room to work here, so be careful.

8. Measure and cut the two boards forming the top and bottom supports.

9. Using glue and 1½" screws countersunk, attach the sides and the back frames to the top and bottom supports. Place at least three screws into the back through the sides. One at the top and bottom and one in the middle. Fill the holes with glue and matching wood plugs and sand flush.

10. Measure and cut the top crown and the bottom foot from the 2" lumber.

11. Rout a ½" cove and lip on the front and sides of the pieces from step 10 using a roman ogee bit and router.

12. Attach the crown and foot at the top and bottom with the routed side facing the frame and about ¼"

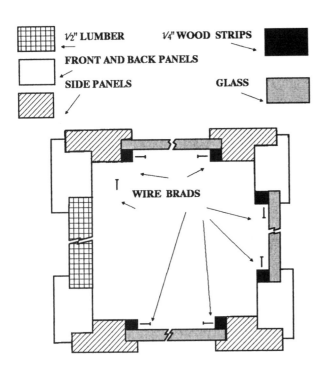

over the front of the side frames. Attach using a screw from the inside of the clock casing through the top and bottom boards into the foot and crown.

13. I suggest that you add an additional foot piece to provide a bottom heavy assembly.

14. Measure and cut the wood pieces forming the clockwork support. This consists of a shelf, support board and two legs. Do this part after you have purchase your works and can verify the positioning of the clock body. You need to make provisions for the pendulum to swing uninhibited and for the weights and chains to hang without rubbing on any surface.

15. Cut two ¾" dados into the clockwork support board to house the leg boards. This should be about ⅜" deep and start 1½" from each end. Cut a ½" dado in the bottom ends of the shelf board.

16. Complete the assembly using screws and glue.

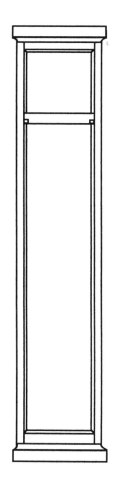

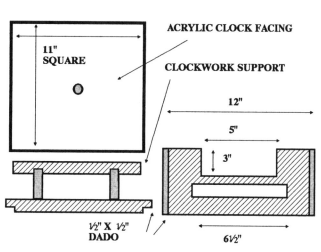

11" SQUARE

ACRYLIC CLOCK FACING

CLOCKWORK SUPPORT

12"

5"

3"

½" X ½" DADO

6½"

17. Measure and cut two support strips and attach as shown on the inside sides of the clock casing. Insert the clockwork support assembly to make certain it fits properly.

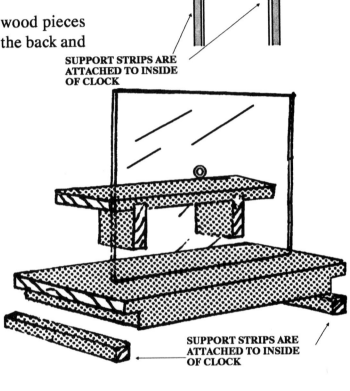

SUPPORT STRIPS ARE ATTACHED TO INSIDE OF CLOCK

18. Measure and cut the wood pieces forming the center of the back and attach using screws and glue.

19. If you plan to cut your own glass do so now, otherwise run down to the store and get the necessary pieces.

SUPPORT STRIPS ARE ATTACHED TO INSIDE OF CLOCK

20. Mortise out the top and bottom corners to fit the depth of the knife hinges. Attach the hinges of the door frame to the front frame and attach to the foot and crown. This piece should fit inside the side frames as shown. Add a small brass knob on the outside and a magnetic latch on the inside.

KNIFE HINGE IS MORTISED INTO DOOR TOP

21. Stain the project now.

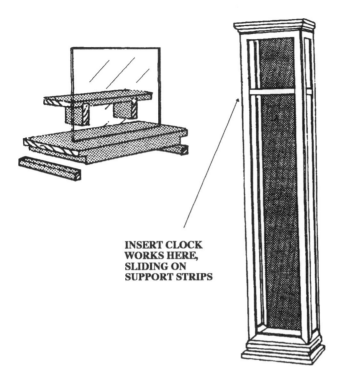

**INSERT CLOCK
WORKS HERE,
SLIDING ON
SUPPORT STRIPS**

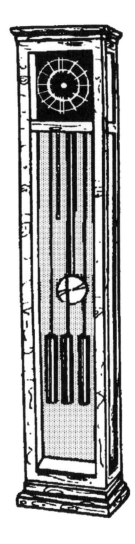

22. Add the glass panels and hold in place with ¼" square strips around the inside butt joined or mitered at the ends. Use ⅝" wire brads and a tack hammer and be extremely careful. Cut the wood strips with a fine toothed back saw mounter in a wood miter box.

23. Drill a ½" hole in the appropriate place of the acrylic sheet and mount to the clockwork's frame as shown. Predrill the screw holes with a countersink so that the screw heads are flush with the sur-

face of the sheet. You may opt to use brass screws for this step.

24. Mount your clockwork and watch time start ticking.

SOURCES OF SUPPLY

The following are direct-mail marketers of clock systems and parts.

KLOCKIT
P.O. BOX 636
Lake Geneva, WI 53147

Mason and Sullivan Co.
586 Higgins Crowell Rd
West Yarmouth, Cape Cod,
MA 02673

The clockwork I used was quite similiar to the Franz Hermle triple-chime movements sold by Mason and Sullivan.

Hanging Sweetheart Lamp

This hanging lamp makes a nice addition to anyone's home. It looks good and casts just enough light to make it a great area illuminator. This will do a nice job over an end table or in a corner of the room as well. The cord is nothing more than plain old macrame over the electric wire and the knots that make it are very simple to do. This is really a great weekend workshop project.

MATERIALS

¾" red oak 6 board feet
   12 pieces 1½" x 16" side boards
   12 pieces 1½" x 4¼" top and
     bottom boards
   1 piece 13" x 15" top
   2 pieces 3" x 6" lamp cord anchor
     boards
   2 pieces 3" x 3" lamp housing sides
   2 pieces 1½" x 3" lamp housing
     ends
   1 piece 3" x 3" lamp housing base
   6 pieces ¾" x 2½" wedges for side
     supports
   24 pieces ⅛" x 1½" x 1" splines

¾" rosewood 1 board foot
   18 pieces ⅛" x 1½" x 13¾" heart
     slats

HARDWARE AND MISCELLANEOUS

24 wood screws 1½" drywall type
24 wood plugs red oak ½"
Carpenter's or Titebond glue
Electric cord for lamp 20 feet
3 ply No. 72 jute macrame cord
  135 feet
8" globe light fixture
1 pint Danish oil walnut

TOOLS REQUIRED

Circular saw
Saber saw
Drill with ½" bit and countersink
  and ¼" bit
Router with cove, rabbet and
  rounding over bits
Screwdriver
Pad sander
Web clamp
Bar or pipe clamps
Chisel ½"

INSTRUCTIONS

1. Measure and cut the wood pieces forming the sides of the hanging lamp. There are six sides each consisting of two long boards with a short top and bottom board.

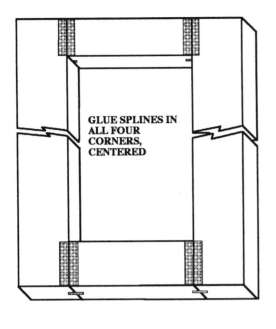

GLUE SPLINES IN ALL FOUR CORNERS, CENTERED

2. Center and cut a saw blade kerf ½" deep and 2" long into the ends of the short boards and into the sides of the ends of each of the long boards.

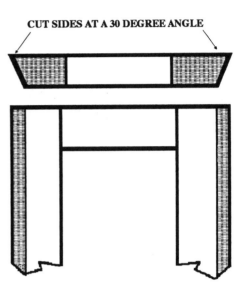

CUT SIDES AT A 30 DEGREE ANGLE

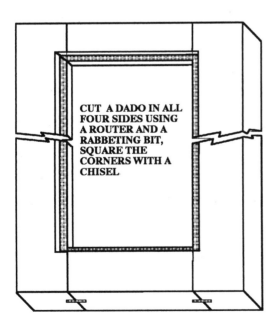

CUT A DADO IN ALL FOUR SIDES USING A ROUTER AND A RABBETING BIT, SQUARE THE CORNERS WITH A CHISEL

3. Assemble the boards into a rectangular shape as shown. Insert thin splines into the ends and clamp and glue into position. Allow the assemblies to dry overnight.

4. Cut the sides of the subassemblies from previous steps to a 30 degree angle as shown. Using a router with a rabbeting bit, rout the inside of the

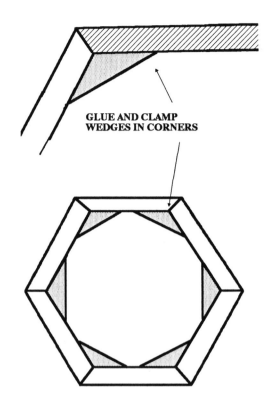

GLUE AND CLAMP WEDGES IN CORNERS

assembly ½" wide and ¼" deep. Square up the corners with a chisel.

5. Assemble all six sides, glue and clamp using a web clamp to hold the structure together. If you don't have a web clamp, you can substitute one with rope and a twist stick, or tie two ends of a rope to a turnbuckle and twist it to apply force. Allow this structure to dry overnight.

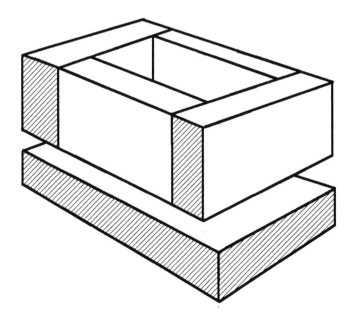

6. Glue small wedges as shown in the bottom corners of each turn. Clamp and allow to dry thoroughly.

7. Measure and cut the lamp housing pieces and screw and glue together. Drill a ½" hole in the center of the base and set aside.

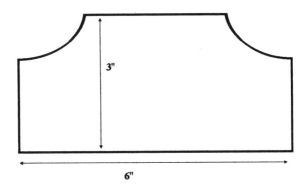

8. The top is cut six-sided just like the basic structure. I sug-

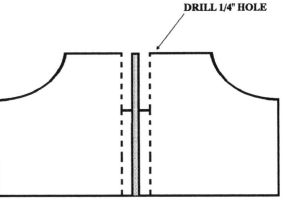

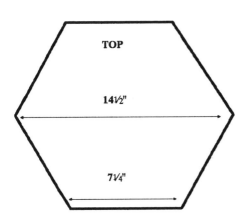

12½" side to side and 14½" tip to tip. You may have to spline two boards to obtain the size you need before cutting the top. Cut the top to size.

gest that you use the structure as a pattern and draw the outline on the board you intend to cut. The top is

9. Measure and cut the lamp cord anchor boards to size. Cut the center so the boards slip over each other forming an +. Rout the edges with a router and a cove bit set to a ¼" depth. Drill two ¼" holes at the top as shown. This is where you will tie

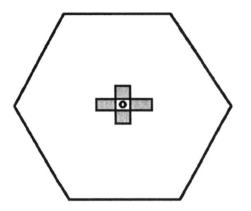

the macrame cords. Drill a ¼" hole down through the center of the +. This hole will allow the lamp cord to go into the lamp.

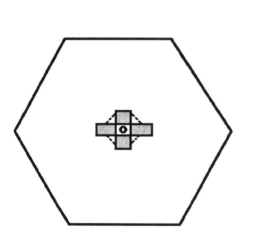

10. Position the + from the last step in the exact center of the top and mark where the center hole should be. Drill a ¼" hole through the top. Position the + and screw from the other side of the top using glue.

11. Position the lamp housing box on the other side of the top and screw in place with screws from the top of the top. Recess the screws and fill the holes with wood plugs, sanding smooth.

A

B

C

12. This next step may be a bit awkward for you if you're a died-in-the-wool woodworker. It's called "how to macrame a half knot and a square knot". Half knot (have not) I know about; I hope a lot of people buy this book so I don't have to say that anymore. Anyhow, here we go. A half knot is usually worked with four macrame cords. The two outer cords are the working cords and the two middle cords are the filler cords:

A. Place the rightmost cord over the filler cord and leave it that way.

B. Next pick up the leftmost cord and place it over the end of the rightmost cord and under the middle cords diagonally so that it ends up through the last space on the right.

C. Pull the two outer cords to tighten. Congratulations, you've just made a half knot.

13. When two or more half knots are tied in sequence, you have a spiraling chain called a half knot sennit. For the second knot, follow the steps outlined above. Keep in mind that your right and left cords will be reversed. If at this point you've decided to throw in the towel, you can always go to the store and buy a metal chain link lamp cord. It won't look as good, but it will work.

14. The next knot, the square knot, starts off as a half knot. Now you know why it is called a half knot. The second step, however, is as

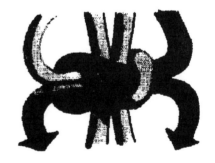

follows:

A. Place what is now the rightmost cord horizontally between the two left cords, leave it in that position.

B. Bring the leftmost cord under the end of the right cord over the middle cords, and through the space between the two right cords.

C. Pull the ends of the outer cords to tighten.

15. When two or more square knots are tied in sequence, the result is a flat chain called a square knot sennit. The macrame chain you are about to develop is made up of a sequence of 5 square knots followed by 15 half knots or a sequence of square knot and half knot sennits. The chain is 15 feet long. You will need 2 cords each 60 feet long, 1 cord 15 feet long and the electric wire 20 feet long. Begin by using the electric wire and the 15 foot cord as the filler cords and the 60 foot cords as the working cords. Make a sennit of 5 square knots followed by a sennit of 15 half knots. Continue alternating this sequence until the working cord is used to the end. Allow a couple of feet of wire at both ends and some extra cord to attach to the lamp. Attach a plug on one end of the electric wire.

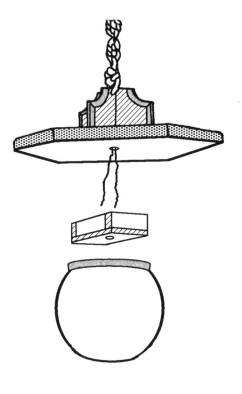

A SQUARE KNOT SENNIT

16. Attach one end of the macrame cord to the top of the lamp housing. Run the electric wire down into the hole in the center. Attach the 8" globe light fixture to the housing and attach the wires to the associated two wires coming down through the center hole.

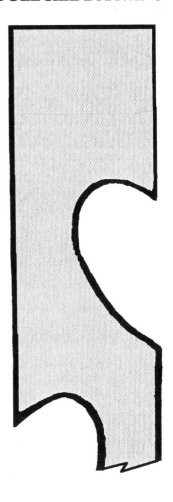

17. The heart cutout pieces can really be made from any contrasting wood. If rosewood is too expensive for your budget, try walnut or some other dark wood. It is best to try and find 2" stock that you can cut into strips. First cut the stock to size, cut out the heart halves and then cut strips ⅛" thick from the

larger stock. Fit these pieces inside the lamp shell and trim to fit the openings. Glue and clamp into position and let dry overnight before proceeding.

18. Attach the lamp top assembly to the top of the shell. Use recessed screws and glue and fill the holes with wood plugs. Sand flush. I used a router to create a cove molding

effect around the top outer edge of the top, which is optional.

19. Stain the lamp the color of your choice. I used a walnut colored Danish oil, which looks good with red oak.

20. Find a favorite spot, hang your lamp, turn it on, stand back and graciously accept all of the applause.

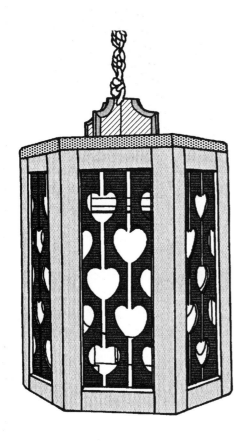

Tavern Lantern and Sconce

Bring a touch of nostalgia into your home with these designs that are reminiscent of projects from times of long ago. These attractive candle holders can be made to hang on the wall or the ceiling or to stand on a shelf. The glow emanating from the center of each lantern or sconce can create a special warm feeling in each room they share.

SCONCE MATERIALS

¾" pine 10" x 48"
    4 pieces ¾" x ¾" x 12" post
    2 pieces &" x 7" inner top and
      bottom
    1 piece 7" x 7" outer bottom
    1 piece 7" x 5½" outer top
    1 piece 2½" diameter insert
    1 piece ¼" x 1" x 3" handle

⅛" clear plastic 12½" x 30"
    4 pieces 6" x 12½"

HARDWARE AND MISCELLANEOUS

12 screws ⅛"
2 screws 1"
12 pieces ½" wood plugs
Carpenter's or Titebond glue
8 finishing nails ½" long
Wood filler
1 pint paint or stain sealer

TOOLS REQUIRED

Hammer
Nail set
Drill with ½" countersink
    and ⅝" spade bit
Circle cutter 2½" diameter
Screwdriver
Saber saw
Circular or table saw
Router with rounding over bit
    and ½" rabbeting bit
Sander pad or belt

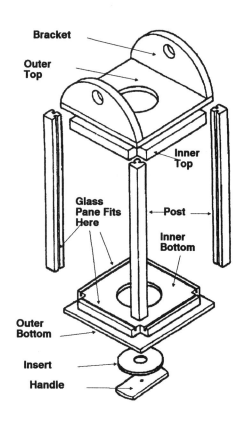

SCONCE INSTRUCTIONS

1. Measure and cut the wood pieces as listed. Cut one long piece ¾" square for the four pieces of post. Do not cut to length yet.

2. Drill a 2½" hole into the center of the top and bottom inner and outer pieces by clamping them together and aligning the center. Save one of the cut outs for the insert. Cut a ½" x 1" slot as shown into opposite sides of the center hole cut into the outer bottom piece.

3. Clamp the inner top and bottom pieces together and cut four ¾" square rabbets in each corner.

4. Cut a ¼" dado ⅛" wide and ⅜" from the outer edge of each side of the inner top and bottom pieces as shown. This is the usual width of a circular saw blade.

5. In the long piece from step 1, cut a ¼" dado ⅛" wide into the center of the two inside edges as shown. Cut the posts to length (12").

6. Drill a ⅝" hole as shown 1" from the top, centered, of the two bracket pieces. Rout both sides of the hole with a rounding over bit and router.

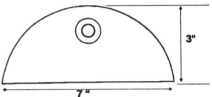

7. Using a router with a ½" rabbeting bit rout the center of the inner bottom to a depth of ⅜" and ½" wide.

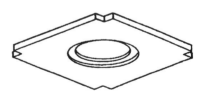

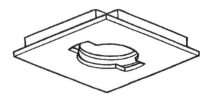

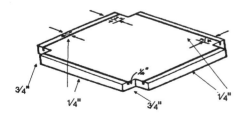

8. Drill four ½" countersunk holes into the bottom and top outer pieces.

9. Drill two ½" countersunk holes into the lower bottom of the brackets, spaced and centered 3" apart and ⅜" from the bottom.

10. Attach the brackets to the outer top creating a 7" x 7" square.

11. Center and attach the outer top and bottom pieces to the inner top and bottom pieces using glue and 1⅛" screws.

12. Drill a ⅝" hole into the center of the insert.

13. Attach the handle to the bottom

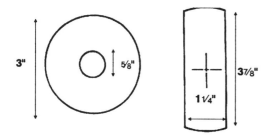

of the insert using glue and two 1" wood screws. Make certain it is centered properly.

14. Measure and cut the four plastic sides from the ⅛" plastic. Do not

remove the protective coating from the plastic until after the pieces are cut to size. The size is 6" x 12½".

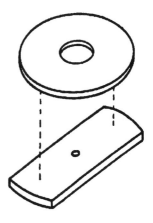

15. If you plan to paint or stain the project, now is the time to do it.

16. Assemble the sconce as shown with the plastic inserts and posts.

17. Put a candle into the insert assembly and gently insert this into the bottom of the sconce, twisting the assembly so it locks into the inner rabbetted ledge.

Tip: I suggest that you glue aluminum foil into the inside top as added insurance against fire.

Remember that these are wood projects designed for show. If you plan to light and use the candles be very careful and watchful for potential fire. Make absolutely certain that the candles are firmly seated into the insert.

TAVERN LANTERN

There are two variations of the tavern lantern. One has a fixed top and the other a removable top with a glass mantle.

MATERIALS

¾" red oak 8" x 48"
- 4 pieces 1½" x 3" top and bottom side pieces (A)
- 2 pieces 1½" x 10" sides (C)
- 2 pieces ¾" x ¾" sides (B)
- 2 pieces 6" x 6" top and bottom (optional)
- 2 pieces 7" x 7" top and bottom
- 1 piece 2½" diameter candle holder

HARDWARE AND MISCELLANEOUS

16 screws 1¼"
8 screws 2"
24 wood plugs ½" red oak
1 piece copper 2½ x 12¹⁄₁₆" thick
6 screws brass ¾"
1 pint Danish oil (dark walnut)
Carpenter's or Titebond glue (substitute clear silicone if you plan to use outdoors).
Glass mantle (optional)
L-shaped curtain hook small (optional)
1 piece leather ¾" x 24" (optional)
12 brads ½" brass (optional)

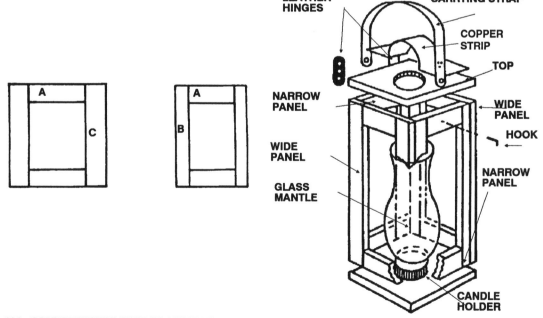

LATCH DETAIL

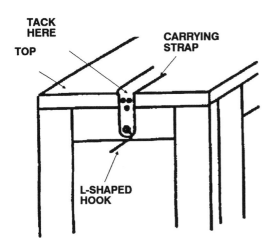

TACK HERE

TOP

CARRYING STRAP

L-SHAPED HOOK

HINGE DETAIL

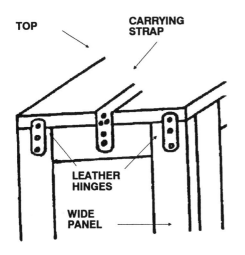

TOP

CARRYING STRAP

LEATHER HINGES

WIDE PANEL

TOOLS REQUIRED

Circular saw
Ball peen hammer
Screwdriver
Drill with ½" countersink bit and
$\quad$ ⅝" spade bit
Circle cutter 2½"

INSTRUCTIONS

1. Measure and cut all of the wood pieces as specified.

2. Drill countersunk holes into the ends of the pieces marked C and B and assemble the sides to the pieces marked A using glue and screws. Attach the two assemblies creating the center assembly as shown.

3. Center and cut a 2½" hole into the top board. Save the cut out for the candle holder.

4. Drill a ⅝" hole into the center of the candle holder.

5. Using a router with a cove bit rout the edges of the top and bottom pieces.

6. Attach the candle holder to the center of the bottom piece and

hold in place with two counter-sunk screws and glue.

7. For a fixed lantern, drill four countersunk holes into the top and bottom pieces and attach them to the center assembly using screws and glue. Glue the wood plugs over the screw holes and sand flush.

8. Measure and cut the copper plate to size. Using a ball peen hammer and an anvil or other hard surface, texture the surface by pounding it with the rounded edge of the hammer.

9. Bend the copper plate as shown and attach it to the top of the tavern lantern using ¾" screws.

10. Stain the project.

WARNING: The brass cover over the top can get very hot. Never touch it while a candle is burning.

These next steps are optional if you want to make the unit with a mantle and removable lid.

1A. Attach the lid using small pieces of leather for hinges as shown. Hold in place with small wire brads.

2A. Cut a small hole in one end of the leather handle and insert it over the curtain hook which is screwed into the front of the top assembly.

3A. Attach the mantle over the candle holder.

Corner China Chest

Corners usually mean wasted space in most houses. This project gives a corner a whole new meaning. This cupboard or hutch, however you wish to refer to it, provides a lot of storage for the dining room or, for that matter, the den. You can store almost anything in it, although it is mostly used for china plates, cups and saucers, hence the name China Chest. No matter what you decide to store in it, it will look good anywhere you put it.

MATERIALS

This cabinet is built in two units, the top and the bottom. It has back boards made from solid lumber, sides from plywood, shelves made from plywood, front boards from solid lumber and two types of doors, one with a wire mesh center and the other with raised panels. It has custom-made molding around the top, middle and bottom, and features curved dowel grapevine at the top, an unusual touch for furniture decoration. You can buy most of the molding pre-made if you do not have access to the equipment to make it.

¾" red oak wood core plywood
   40 board feet
   1 piece 17" x 38" lower cabinet top
   1 piece upper cabinet top 17" x 38"
   2 pieces 17" x 38" upper cabinet shelf
   1 piece 17" x 38" lower cabinet shelf
   1 piece 17" x 38" lower cabinet floor
   1 piece 19" x 38" upper cabinet floor
   1 piece 14" x 38" upper cabinet back
   1 piece 14" x 30" lower cabinet back

1x12 red oak lumber 16 board feet
   2 pieces 6⅜" x 38" upper cabinet front
   2 pieces 2¼" x 38" upper cabinet facer
   2 pieces 2¼" x 30" vertical facer lower cabinet
   2 pieces 2¼" x 25⅝" horizontal facer lower cabinet
   2 pieces 2" x 12¾" upper door rail
   2 pieces 2" x 36⅜" upper door stiles
   2 pieces 2" x 12¾" lower door rails
   2 pieces 2" x 28⅞" lower door stiles
   2 pieces 9⅜" x 23½" lower door panels
   1 piece 2½" x 48" cut to size top panel trim for grapevine
   2 pieces 1⅜" x8" lip trim

Molding red oak assorted sizes and shapes
   1 piece 1" x 48" cove and bead
   1 pieces 1" x 48" flute and bead
   1 piece 2" x 48" bead
   1 piece 3" x 48" cove and bead
   1 piece 3¼" x 100" bead
   1 piece ½" x 48" cove and bead
   1 piece 2" x 48" mitered bead molding

¼" red oak plywood 20 board feet
- 2 pieces 18⅛" x 38" upper cabinet sides
- 2 pieces 18⅛" x 30" lower cabinet sides
- 2 pieces ½" x 9¾" and
- 2 pieces ½" x 32⅜" upper door backing

2x2 white pine 8 linear feet
- 1 piece 30" and 2 pieces 5" bottom front molding support
- 2 pieces 17" side molding support
- 1 piece 13" back molding support

1x4 white pine 3 linear feet

HARDWARE AND MISCELLANEOUS

- 10 feet wood dowel ¼"
- 4 hinges H variety brass
- 4 door pulls brass
- 4 door latches magnetic
- 1 piece 24" x 36" decorative brass wire mesh
- 100 wood screws 1½" drywall type
- Carpenter's or Titebond glue
- 1 quart Danish oil walnut
- 100 wood plugs red oak ½"
- box ¾" wire brads

TOOLS REQUIRED

Table saw
Drill with countersink
Screwdriver
Wire cutters
Router with ¼" and ½" straight bits, cove and bead, sash, flute and ogee bits
Hammer

INSTRUCTIONS

1. Measure and cut the pieces forming the shelves, top and bottom pieces for the upper and lower cabinet. Note: If you do not want the wood core edge to show on the shelving, cut the front ½" shorter. Cut a facing board ½" wide and the length of the front from the red oak stock and tack and glue in place. I also cut a decora-

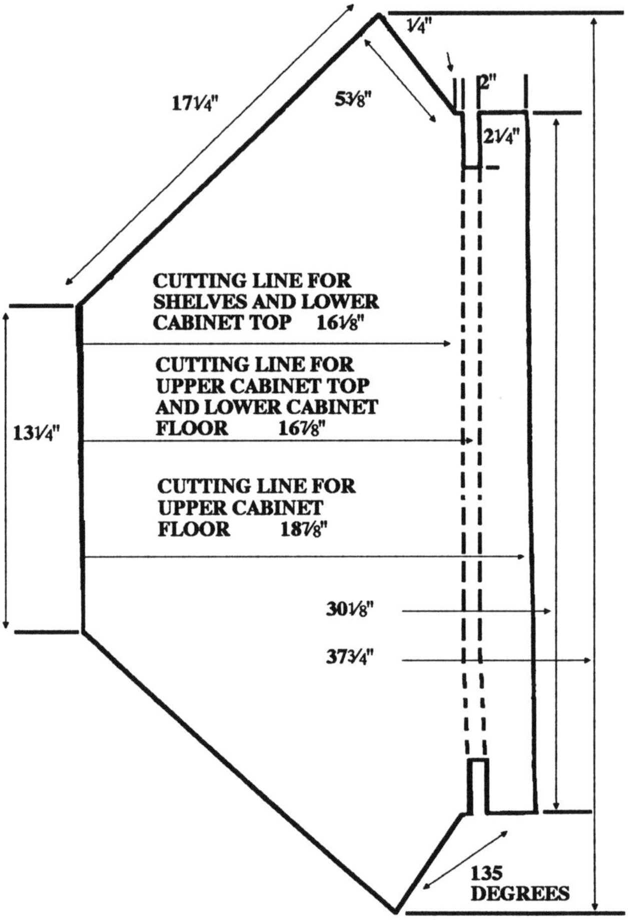

17¼"
5⅜"
¼"
2"
2¼"
CUTTING LINE FOR SHELVES AND LOWER CABINET TOP 16⅛"
CUTTING LINE FOR UPPER CABINET TOP AND LOWER CABINET FLOOR 16⅞"
CUTTING LINE FOR UPPER CABINET FLOOR 18⅞"
13¼"
30⅛"
37¾"
135 DEGREES

SHELF DECORATIVE MOLDING CUT

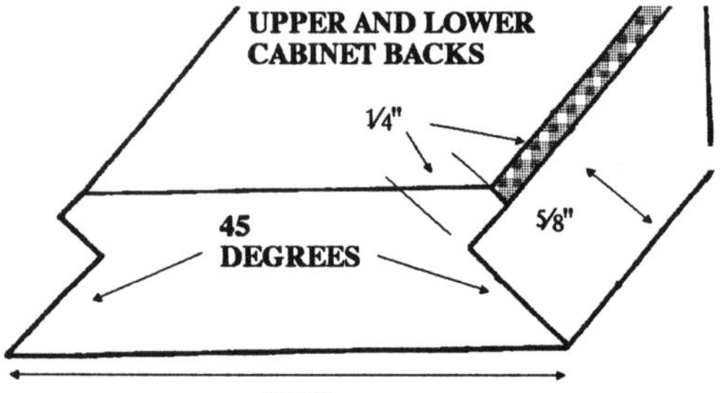

UPPER AND LOWER CABINET BACKS
¼"
⅝"
45 DEGREES
13¼"

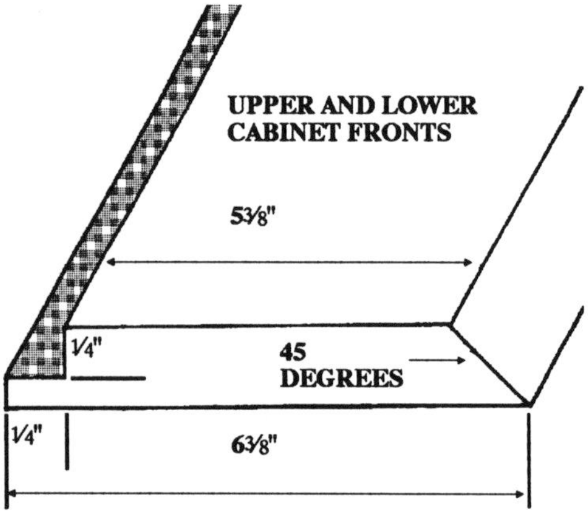

UPPER AND LOWER CABINET FRONTS
5⅜"
¼"
45 DEGREES
¼"
6⅜"

tive mold in the front of the shelves.

2. Measure and cut the back, sides, front and facer boards from the plywood and red oak lumber. The back boards must have a 45 degree dado as shown to accommodate the ¼" plywood sides. The front boards need a ¼" dado on one side and a 45 degree miter on the end as shown.

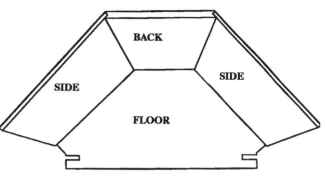

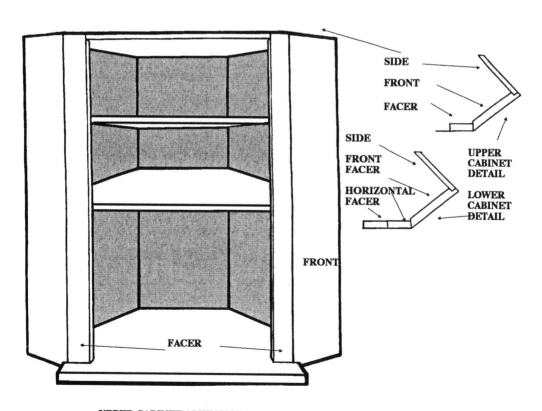

UPPER CABINET ASSEMBLY

3. Assemble the top cabinet by wrapping the top and bottom and shelves with the plywood sides and back and the wood pieces in the front. Space the cabinet shelves evenly or as you choose. Attach the plywood sides using glue and wire brads. Attach the other pieces using countersunk screws. Glue the top flush with the other boards.

4. Assemble the lower cabinet much in the same way as the upper unit except that it has two horizontal facing boards that should be installed at the top and bottom to complete the lower unit door frame.

5. The upper and lower door frames are assembled in the same method with stiles and rails with ⅜" lap cuts. Glue the upper cabinet door boards and allow them to dry overnight before proceeding.

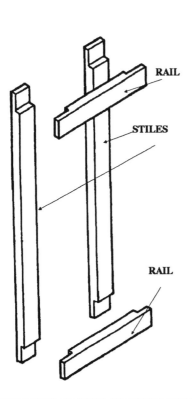

RAIL

STILES

RAIL

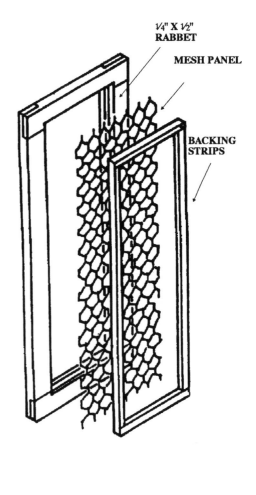

¼" X ½"
RABBET

MESH PANEL

BACKING
STRIPS

6. The upper doors are rabbeted on the inside edge as shown to accommodate the wire mesh. Cut the wire mesh to size and put in place with the ¼" plywood backing. Hold in place with glue and wire brads.

7. The lower doors need a ¼" wide and ⅜" deep dado cut in the inside center to accommodate the panel. This is best done with a router and a ¼" slot cutter or a dado blade in a table saw.

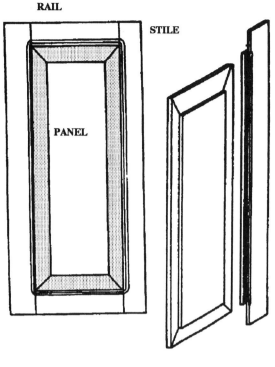

RAIL

STILE

PANEL

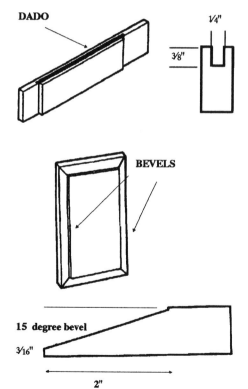

DADO

¼"

⅜"

BEVELS

15 degree bevel

³⁄₁₆"

2"

8. Measure and cut the lower unit door panels to size. Cut a 15 degree bevel 2" deep on the sides forming the raised panel. You can do this with a table saw or a raised panel cutter in a router mounted securely in a router table. Cut the bevel so the tip or edge of the panel is slightly less than ¼".

9. Assemble the lower door by gluing the rails and stiles together with the panel floating free inside the dado cut. Do not glue the panel in place.

10. Measure and cut the lip trim and glue and screw in place, aligned with the front of the upper cabinet floor.

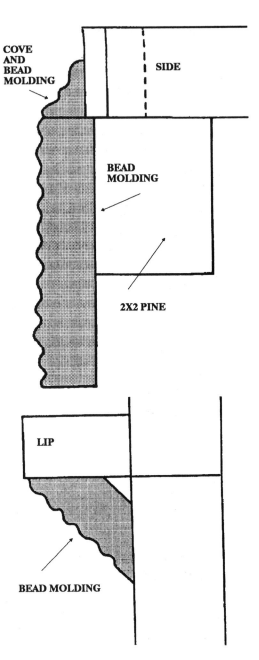

COVE AND BEAD MOLDING

SIDE

BEAD MOLDING

2X2 PINE

LIP

BEAD MOLDING

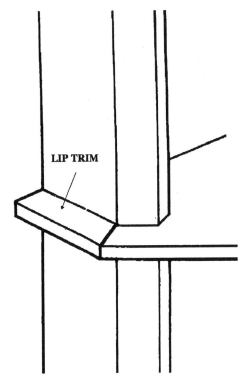

LIP TRIM

11. Run the 2" pine around the bottom of the lower cabinet and face with the 3" bead molding. Cap this with the narrow cove and bead molding. Continue to run the 3" molding along the inside of the sides and back so that its face is flush with the edge of the floor of the lower cabinet.

12. Measure and cut the mitered edge bead molding and run it around the bottom edge of the upper cabinet floor facing and the lip trim. This can get tricky, as a compound miter must be cut.

13. Measure and cut the various molding pieces forming a sandwich across the top of the upper cabinet as shown. Start with the 3" cove and bead followed by the 2" bead. On top of this, place the grape vine board followed by the flute and bead and cove and bead molding pieces. I suggest that you do this on top of your workbench and then mount to the top of the cabinet. The last part of this decorative piece is the formation of the grapevine trim. Use screws and glue to complete this assembly.

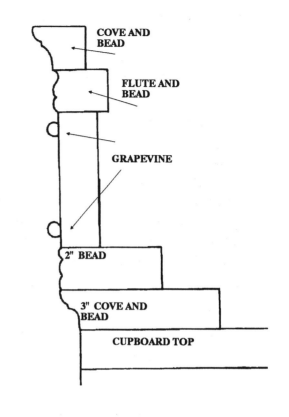

COVE AND BEAD

FLUTE AND BEAD

GRAPEVINE

2" BEAD

3" COVE AND BEAD

CUPBOARD TOP

14. Soak the ¼" wood dowel in water for about three days. Cut ten shaping blocks from the 1x4 pine lumber. Tack the shaping blocks along the front of the panel as shown, about ½" apart. Take a full length of wood dowel, and, beginning in the center of the form and dowel, bend the wood dowel to conform to the shape of the shaping blocks. Notch

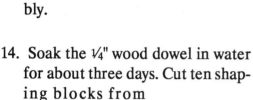

SHAPING BLOCKS

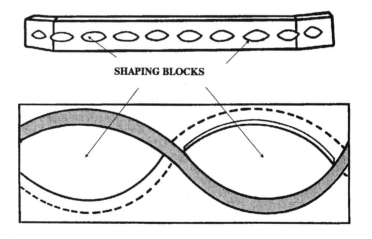

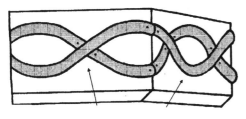

GRAPEVINE DETAIL

the pieces using a small pocket knife where they overlap. Hold in place with wire brads. When the dowel has dried, remove it and the shaping blocks. Put wood filler in the brad holes and sand flush. Reattach the dowel forms using

wire brads and glue. Recess the brad heads and fill the holes with wood filler and sand flush. Note: you may prefer to do the dowel forming task on a form laid out on top of your workbench.

15. Attach the doors to the top and bottom cabinets using decorative H hinges. Attach brass door pulls or knobs and install magnetic door catches at the top and bottom.

16. Stain the project the color of your choice and go get a cool one.

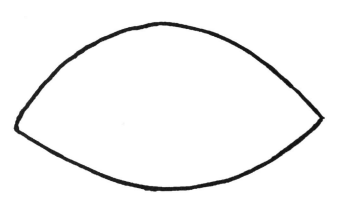

SHAPING BLOCK FULL SIZE PATTERN

One Final Note

I hope that you enjoyed building these projects as well as the other projects from my syndicated newspaper columns and PBS programs. If you need full size patterns, or if you would like to see some of the other projects we make, send $3.00 for our catalog. If you have any questions about this book, or if you need help, write to my attention, and we will get back to you as soon as possible. Our address is:

The Weekend Workshop
P.O. Box 40
Eureka, Missouri 63025

And remember, you really can make it!

Index

B

bench and chest combination,
173-180
  armrest assembly, 180
  backrest facing, 178
  base and floor, 175
  base frame, 175
  box with top facing, 176
  hardware and miscellaneous,
  175
  illustration of, 180
  inner frame, 176
  instructions, 175-180
  materials, 174
  seat with corner facings, 177
  seat with front trim board, 178
  splined sides, 176
  tools required, 175
bevels, 5-6
birdhouse cookie jar, 29-36
  hardware and miscellaneous, 31
  illustration of, 36
  instructions, 31-36
  materials, 30
  tools required, 31
biscuit joints, 6-9
blanket chest, 153-160
  chest side, 156
  floor, adding of, 157
  front trim, 156
  front, adding of, 157
  hardware and miscellaneous,
  154
  illustration of, 159
  instructions, 154-160
  left side of back, 155
  lid assembly, 158
  materials, 154
  notes and calculations, 160
  side brace, adding of, 157
  side to back, attaching of, 157
  tools required, 154

bread box, 127-134
  hardware and miscellaneous,
  128
  illustration of, 133
  instructions, 128-134
  materials, 128
  notes and calculations, 134
  side view, 129
  tools required, 128
breakfast nook, 181-194
  benches, instructions for,
  188-194
  finishing the projects, 192-193
  hardware and miscellaneous,
  182
  illustration of, 193
  materials, 182
  notes and calculations, 194
  table, instructions for, 183-188
  tools required, 183
breakfast nook benches, 188-194
  instructions, 188-194
breakfast nook table, 183-188
  instructions, 183-188
bunny bandit and calico gal wall
  hanging, 135-140
  bunny pattern, 139
  frame measurement, 140
  hardware and miscellaneous,
  136
  illustration of, 137
  instructions, 136-140
  materials, 136
  tools required, 136
butt joints, 4

C

calendar clock, 195-200
  clock face, 200
  face and months, making of,
  199-200

hardware and miscellaneous,
  196
  instructions, 198-200
  main components, 197
  materials, 196
  month facing, 200
  tools required, 196
chairs and rockers, 71-82
  hardware and miscellaneous, 73
  instructions, 74-82
  materials, 72-73
  rocker bending frame, 80
  seat top view, 79
  tools required, 74
chairs, 71-82
checkerboard game and coffee
  table, 37-44
  hardware and miscellaneous, 38
  illustration of, 43
  instructions, 38-44
  feet and legs, instructions,
  40-41
  game top, instructions, 39
  materials, 38
  notes and calculations, 44
  tools required, 38
child's rocker/doll cradle combo,
  89-98
  armrest and support, 93
  cradle foot, 92
  cradle head, 92
  cradle subassembly, 95
  hardware and miscellaneous, 90
  illustration of, 97
  instructions, 91-97
  materials, 90
  notes and calculations, 98
  rocker and braces placement, 93
  tools required, 90
china chest, 229-238
  hardware and miscellaneous,
  231

china chest (*Cont.*)
  illustration of, 231
  instructions, 232-238
  materials, 230-231,
  shaping block pattern, 238
  tools required, 231
  upper cabinet assembly, 233
chopping block/serving cart,
  105-118
  bin assembly, 113
  bin pivot block installation, 114
  bin stop installation, 114
  hardware and miscellaneous,
    106
  illustration of, 115
  instructions, 107-118
  leg assembly, 110
  materials, 106
  notes and calculations, 118
  shelf assembly, 110
  shelf installation, 112
  tools required, 106
coffee table, 37-44
  hardware and miscellaneous, 38
  illustration of, 43
  instructions, 38-44
  feet and legs, instructions,
    40-41
  game top, instructions, 39
  materials, 38
  notes and calculations, 44
  tools required, 38
cookie jar, 29-36
  hardware and miscellaneous, 31
  illustration of, 36
  instructions, 31-36
  materials, 30
  tools required, 31
corner china chest, 229-238
  hardware and miscellaneous, 231
  illustration of, 231
  instructions, 232-238
  materials, 230-231,
  shaping block pattern, 238
  tools required, 231
  upper cabinet assembly, 233
corner shelves, 83-88
  facing size, 85
  hardware and miscellaneous, 84
  illustration of, 87
  inserts, 86
  instructions, 84-88
  materials, 84
  notes and calculations, 88
country footstool, 13-18

hardware and miscellaneous, 14
instructions, 14-17
leg assembly, instructions,
  16-17
materials, 14
notes and calculations, 17
seat base, instructions, 14-15
tools required, 14
country modern grandfather
  clock, 201-210
  hardware and miscellaneous,
    203
  instructions, 203-210
  materials, 202-203
  sources of supply, 210
  tools required, 203
curved-back chairs and rockers,
  71-82
  hardware and miscellaneous, 73
  instructions, 74-82
  materials, 72-73
  rocker bending frame, 80
  seat top view, 79
  tools required, 74

D

dadoes, 5
deacon's bench and chest
  combination, 173-180
  armrest assembly, 180
  backrest facing, 178
  base and floor, 175
  base frame, 175
  box with top facing, 176
  hardware and miscellaneous,
    175
  illustration of, 180
  inner frame, 176
  instructions, 175-180
  materials, 174
  seat with corner facings, 177
  seat with front trim board, 178
  splined sides, 176
  tools required, 175
door harp, 99-104
  hardware and miscellaneous,
    100
  illustration of, 104
  instructions, 101-104
  materials, 100
  tools required, 101
dry sink, 161-168
  base with top, assembly of, 164
  door assembly, 166
  finished top, 166

finishing the project, 167
front and side molding, 167
hardware and miscellaneous,
  162
instructions, 163-168
materials, 162
notes and calculations, 168
tools required, 163
top and bottom frames, 163
top assembly, 164
top with back, assembly of, 165

E

early American dry sink, 161-168
  base with top, assembly of, 164
  door assembly, 166
  finished top, 166
  finishing the project, 167
  front and side molding, 167
  hardware and miscellaneous,
    162
  instructions, 163-168
  materials, 162
  notes and calculations, 168
  tools required, 163
  top and bottom frames, 163
  top assembly, 164
  top with back, assembly of, 165

F

final note, 239
finishes, 9-10
footstool, country, 13-18
forever calendar clock, 195-200
  clock face, 200
  face and months, making of,
    199-200
  hardware and miscellaneous,
    196
  instructions, 198-200
  main components, 197
  materials, 196
  month facing, 200
  tools required, 196

G

game table/cabinet, 141-148
  facing, addition of, 144
  front and door assembly, 146
  hardware and miscellaneous,
    142
  illustration of, 148
  instructions, 142-148
  materials, 142
  molding attachment, 144

saw kerfs, 145
side attachment, 143
spade pattern, 146
tools required, 142
glue joints, 6-9
  adhesives, 8
  hardware for, 8
  screws and nails for, 8-9
grandfather clock, 201-210
  hardware and miscellaneous, 203
  instructions, 203-210
  materials, 202-203
  sources of supply, 210
  tools required, 203

H

hanging lamp, 211-220
  hardware and miscellaneous, 212
  illustration of, 220
  instructions, 212-220
  macrame cords, 216-218
  materials, 212
  tools required, 212
hanging sweetheart lamp, 211-220
  hardware and miscellaneous, 212
  illustration of, 220
  instructions, 212-220
  macrame cords, 216-218
  materials, 212
  tools required, 212

K

kitchen and patio chopping block/serving cart, 105-118
  bin assembly, 113
  bin pivot block installation, 114
  bin stop installation, 114
  hardware and miscellaneous, 106
  illustration of, 115
  instructions, 107-118
  leg assembly, 110
  materials, 106
  notes and calculations, 118
  shelf assembly, 110
  shelf installation, 112
  tools required, 106

L

lap desk, 169-172
  hardware and miscellaneous, 170
  instructions, 170-172
  lip of lid, 172
  materials, 170
  sides, 171
  tools required, 170
lap joints, 5

M

macrame cords, 216-218
magazine rack, 149-152
  hardware and miscellaneous, 150
  instructions, 151-152
  materials, 150
  tool required, 150
magazine rack and tissue dispenser, 23-28
  hardware and miscellaneous, 24
  instructions, 24-27
  materials, 24
  notes and calculations, 28
  tools required, 24
mirror and change holder, 10-22
  hardware and miscellaneous, 19
  instructions, 21-22
  materials, 19
  tools required, 19
mirror, 10-22, 18
  sweetheart, 10-22, 18
mirrored candle sconces, 49-54
  bracket, 51
  candle holder, 52
  completed assembly, 52
  hardware and miscellaneous, 50
  illustration of, 53
  instructions, 50-54
  materials, 50
  notes and calculations, 54
  shelf, 51
  tools required, 50
miters and bevels, 5-6
miters, 5-6
mortise and tenon joints, 5

P

paper cup dispenser, 55-58
  hardware and miscellaneous, 56
  instructions, 56-58
  materials, 56
  tools required, 56
patterns, working with, 10-11
plate and cup rack, 59-62
  bracket, instructions, 60
  hardware and miscellaneous, 60
  illustration of, 62
  instructions, 60-62
  materials, 60
  tools required, 60
preservatives, 9-10

R

rabbet joints, 4-5
rocker bending frame, 80
rocker/cradle combo, 89-98
  armrest and support, 93
  cradle foot, 92
  cradle head, 92
  cradle subassembly, 95
  hardware and miscellaneous, 90
  illustration of, 97
  instructions, 91-97
  materials, 90
  notes and calculations, 98
  rocker and braces placement, 93
  tools required, 90
rockers, 71-82
rolltop bread box, 127-134
  hardware and miscellaneous, 128
  illustration of, 133
  instructions, 128-134
  materials, 128
  notes and calculations, 134
  side view, 129
  tools required, 128

S

saw kerfs, 145
sconces, 49-54
  bracket, 51
  candle holder, 52
  completed assembly, 52
  hardware and miscellaneous, 50
  illustration of, 53
  instructions, 50-54
  materials, 50
  notes and calculations, 54
  shelf, 51
  tools required, 50
settle, 119-126
  hardware and miscellaneous, 121
  illustration of, 125
  instructions, 121-126
  lower front design, 122
  materials, 120
  notes and calculations, 126

settle (*Cont.*)
  tools required, 121
  two versions, 123
settle/toy chest, 63-70
  floor and seat supports, 67
  front bottom of chest, 66
  hardware and miscellaneous, 64
  illustration of, 69
  instructions, 64-70
  materials, 64
  notes and calculations, 70
  tools required, 64
shadow box 45-48
  hardware and miscellaneous, 46
  back, instructions for, 48
  bottom, instructions for, 48
  complete assembly, instructions
    for, 47
  shelves, instructions for, 47
  side, instructions for, 48
  top, instructions for, 46
  instructions, 46-48
  materials, 46
  tools required, 46
spline glue joints, 6-9
sweetheart door harp, 99-104
  hardware and miscellaneous,
    100
  illustration of, 104
  instructions, 101-104
  materials, 100
  tools required, 101
sweetheart magazine rack,
    149-152
  hardware and miscellaneous,
    150
  instructions, 151-152
  materials, 150
  tool required, 150
sweetheart mirror and change
    holder, 10-22
  hardware and miscellaneous, 19
  instructions, 21-22
  materials, 19
  tools required, 19
sweetheart settle, 119-126
  hardware and miscellaneous,
    121
  illustration of, 125
  instructions, 121-126
  lower front design, 122
  materials, 120
  notes and calculations, 126
  tools required, 121
  two versions, 123

sweetheart shadow box, 45-48
  hardware and miscellaneous, 46
  back, instructions for, 48
  bottom, instructions for, 48
  complete assembly, instructions
    for, 47
  shelves, instructions for, 47
  side, instructions for, 48
  top, instructions for, 46
  instructions, 46-48
  materials, 46
  tools required, 46

T
table/cabinet, 141-148
  facing, addition of, 144
  front and door assembly, 146
  hardware and miscellaneous,
    142
  illustration of, 148
  instructions, 142-148
  materials, 142
  molding attachment, 144
  saw kerfs, 145
  side attachment, 143
  spade pattern, 146
  tools required, 142
tavern lantern and sconce,
    221-228
  lantern, 226-228
    hardware and miscellaneous,
    226
    hinge detail, 227
    illustration of, 228
    instructions, 227-228
    latch detail, 227
    materials, 226
    tools required, 227
  sconce, 222-225
    hardware and miscellaneous,
    222
    illustration of, 225
    instructions, 223-225
    materials, 222
    tools required, 222
teddy bear settle/toy chest, 63-70
  floor and seat supports, 67
  front bottom of chest, 66
  hardware and miscellaneous, 64
  illustration of, 69
  instructions, 64-70
  materials, 64
  notes and calculations, 70
  tools required, 64
tips and techniques, 1-12

  notes and calculations, 12
  patterns, working with, 10-11
  preservatives and finishes, 9-10
  selecting wood, 2-3
  wood grades, 3-4
  wood joining, 4-9
  woodworking, 1-12
toy chest, 63-70
  floor and seat supports, 67
  front bottom of chest, 66
  hardware and miscellaneous, 64
  illustration of, 69
  instructions, 64-70
  materials, 64
  notes and calculations, 70
  tools required, 64
tulip motif breakfast nook,
    181-194
  benches, instructions, 188-194
  finishing the projects, 192-193
  hardware and miscellaneous,
    182
  illustration of, 193
  materials, 182
  notes and calculations, 194
  table, instructions, 183-188
  tools required, 183

W
wall hanging, 135-140
  bunny pattern, 139
  frame measurement, 140
  hardware and miscellaneous,
    136
  illustration of, 137
  instructions, 136-140
  materials, 136
  tools required, 136
wood grades, 3-4
wood joining, 4-9
  butt joints, 4
  dadoes, 5
  lap joints, 5
  mortise and tenon joints, 5
  rabbets, 4-5
  splines, dowels and biscuit
    joints, 6-9
wood, 2-4
  grades of, 3-4
  hardwood, 2
  selection of, 2-3
  softwood, 2-3
woodworking tips and techniques,
    1-12